Aleksandr Sergeevich Pushkin, Charles Edward Turner

Translations from Poushkin in Memory of the hundredth Anniversary of the Poet's Birthday

Aleksandr Sergeevich Pushkin, Charles Edward Turner

Translations from Poushkin in Memory of the hundredth Anniversary of the Poet's Birthday

ISBN/EAN: 9783337188498

Printed in Europe, USA, Canada, Australia, Japan

Cover: Foto ©ninafisch / pixelio.de

More available books at **www.hansebooks.com**

TRANSLATIONS

FROM

POUSHKIN.

TRANSLATIONS

FROM

POUSHKIN

IN MEMORY OF

THE HUNDREDTH ANNIVERSARY

OF THE

POET'S BIRTHDAY.

BY

CHARLES EDWARD TURNER

English Lector in the University of St. Petersburg.

ST. PETERSBURG.		LONDON.
K. L. RICKER, NEVSKY PROSPECT, № 14.		SAMPSON LOW, MARSTON & COMPANY, LIMITED.

1899.

Permis par la censure, St-Pétersbourg, le 30 mars 1899.
Imprimerie Trenké et Fusnot, Maximilianovsky pér., № 13.

CONTENTS.

I. Shorter Poems:
    1. The Dreamer 3
    2. The Grave of a Youth 6
    3. I have Outlived my every Wish 8
    4. To the Sea. 8
    5. Elegy 11
    6. Vain Gift, Gift of Chance 11
    7. Drowned. 12
    8. The Unwashed. 15
    9. A Winter Morning 17
    10. The Noisy Joys of Thoughtless Years are Spent. 18
    11. A Study 19
    12. To the Calumniators of Russia 20
    13. The Poet 22
    14. God grant, my reason ne'er Betray me 22
    15. My Monument 24
II. The Gipsies, a poem 27
III. Poltava, a poem in three cantos 55
IV. Mozart and Saglieri, a dramatic sketch 109
V. The Bronze Cavalier, a poem in two cantos . . . 125
VI. The Statue Guest, a dramatic sketch 145
VII. Boris Godounoff, an historical tragedy 187
VIII. Explanatory notes 305

ERRATA.

Page 14: line 22. For trough, read *through*.
„ 36: „ 17. „ grol wimpatient, read *growl impatient*.
„ 79: „ 6. „ tho, read *the*.
„ 177: „ 12. „ heark, read *hark*.
„ 239: „ 19. „ langhter, read *laughter*.
„ 289: „ 2. „ graut, read *grant*.

*The whispers sweet of liberty and love
Inspired my open soul with simple song;
The poet's muse, a venal slave to none,
Became an echo of our people's voice.*

POUSHKIN.

TO HIS FORMER AND ACTUAL PUPILS

OF

THE IMPERIAL ALEXANDER LYCEUM

THIS LITTLE VOLUME IS DEDICATED

BY

THEIR OLD FRIEND AND WELL-WISHER,

The Translator.

SHORTER POEMS.

THE DREAMER.

The moon pursues her stealthy course,
    The shades grow gray upon the hill,
Silence has fallen on the stream,
    Fresh from the valley blows the wind;
The songster of spring days has hushed
    His notes in waste of gloomy groves,
The herds are couched along the fields,
    And calm the flight of midnight hour.

And night the peaceful ingle-nook
    Has with her misty livery clad;
In stove the flames have ceased to dart,
    And candle down to socket burned;
The saintly face of household gods
    Now darkly gloom from modest shrine,
And taper pale in dimness burns
    Before the guardians of home.

With head in hand bent lowly down,
    In sweet forgetfulness deep plunged,
I lose myself in fancy dreams,
    And lie awake on lonely couch;

As with the weird dark shades of night,
    Illumined by the soft moon's rays,
Wingèd dreams, in hurrying crowds,
    Flock down and strongly seize my soul.

And now flows forth a soft, soft voice,
    The golden chords in music tremble;
And in the hour when all is still,
    The dreamer young begins his song,
With secret ache of soul possessed
    And dreams that come from God alone,
With flying hand he boldly smites
    The breathing strings of heavenly lyre.

Blessed is he who, born in lowly hut,
    Prays not for fortune or for wealth;
From him great Jove, with watchful eyes,
    Will turn mishap that teems with ruin;
At eve, on lotos flowers couched,
    He lies enwrapped in softest sleep;
Nor harshest sound of warrior's trump
    Has power to stir him from his dream.

Let glory, with her daring front,
    Strike loudly on her noisy shield;
In vain she tempts me from afar,
    With skinny finger red in blood;
In vain war's gaudy banners float,
    Or battle-ranks their pomp display;
Peace has higher charms for gentle heart,
    Nor do I care for glory's prize.

In solitude my blood is tamed,
    And tranquilly the days pass by:
From God I have the gift of song,
    Of gifts the rarest, most divine;
And never has the Muse betrayed me:
    Be thou with me, oh goddess dear,
The vilest home or desert wild
    Shall have a beauty of their own.

In dusky dawn of golden days
    The untried singer thou hast blessed,
As with a wreath of myrtle fresh
    Thou didst encrown his childish brow,
And, bringing with thee light from heaven,
    Radiant made his humble cell;
And, gently breathing, thou didst lean
    O'er his cradle with blessing sweet.

For ever be my friend and guide
    Even to the threshold of the grave!
O'er me hover with gentlest dreams,
    And shroud me with thy shielding wings!
Banish far all doubt and sorrow,
    Possess the mind with fond deceit,
A glory shed o'er my far life,
    And scatter wide its darkest gloom!

Thus peace shall bless my parting hour,
    The genius of Death shall come,
And whisper, knocking at the door,
    „The dwelling of the shades awaits thee!"

E'en so, on winter eve sweet sleep
  Frequents with joy the home of peace,
With lotos crowned, and lowly bent
  On restful staff of languid ease.

THE GRAVE OF A YOUTH.

The world he fled,
Of love and pleasure once the nursling,
And is as one who lies in sleep,
Or cold of nameless tomb, forgot.

Time was, he loved our village games,
When as the girls beneath the shade
Of trees would foot the meadow free;
But now in village song and dance
No more is heard his greeting light.

His elders had with envy marked
His easy gait and bearing gay,
And, smiling sadly, 'mongst themselves
Oft shook their hoary heads, and said:
„We too once loved the choral dance,
And shone as wits and jesters keen;
But wait: the years will make their round.
And thou shalt be what we are now.
Be taught by us, life's jocund guest,
The world to thee will soon prove cold:
Thou now mayst dance!".... The elders live,
Whilst he, in ripest bloom of youth,
Has, fading, perished ere his time.

Wild the feast, and loud the song,
Although his voice is ever mute;
New friends now fill the vacant seat;
Seldom, seldom, when maidens chat,
And talk of love, his name is spoke;
Of all, whose hearts his words made flame,
It may be, one will shed a tear,
As memory recalls some scene
Of joy long buried in his grave.....
And wherefore weep?

            Bathed by a stream,
In calm array, the lines of tombs,
Each guarded by its wooden cross,
Lie hidden in the antique grove,
There, close beside the highroad's edge,
Where old beech-trees their branches wave,
His heart at peace and free from care,
Sleeps his last sleep the gentle youth.

In vain, the light of day pours down,
Or morn from mid-sky shines full bright,
Or, splashing round the senseless tomb,
The river purls, or forest wails;
In vain, at early morn, in quest
Of berries red, the village maid
Shall to the stream her basket bring,
And, frightened, dip her naked foot
Into the cold spring-waters fresh;
No sound can wake, or call him forth
The silent walls of his sad grave.

I HAVE OUTLIVED MY EVERY WISH.

I have outlived my every wish,
  Each dear dream seen rudely broken,
And naught remains but woe and plaint,
  Sole heritage of vacant heart.

Despoiled by storms of jealous fate,
  The tree of life has faded fast;
I live in grief and loneliness,
  And wait in hope, the end may come.

As when the last, forgotten leaf,
  That quivers on the naked branch,
By nipping frost is sudden caught,
  And shriek of winter's storm is heard.

TO THE SEA.

  Farewell, thou free, all — conquering sea!
No more wilt thou before me roll
In endless flow thy dark-blue billows
And revel in thy beauty proud.

  Like mournful voice of friend departing,
Like summons sad to bid adieu,
Thy murmur soft from region far
I hearken, but shall hear no more.

For thou hast been my soul's desired bound,
As oft along thy pebbly shore
With slow and measured step I wandered,
And gladly lost in thoughts mine own.

How I have loved thy mystic echoes;
Dull sounds, a voice from the abyss;
In evening hour, thy peaceful ripple.
Thy wayward bursts of sudden rage!

In fragile boat the fisher sailing
Thou lovst to shield from wave's caprice,
And safe it skims o'er surging breakers;
But with unconquered strength wilt rise,
And vessel proud to pieces dash.

Too long, a willing slave, I have served,
Removed from thee, a sordid world;
Too long forgot with song to greet thee,
And o'er thy crested waves to waft
My verse sonorous and sincere.

Thou didst wait, thou didst call, but a spell
My vainly struggling soul subdued;
Enchanted by a mighty passion,
I still remained from thee estranged.

But why complain? Whither now should I
My vain and aimless steps direct?
O'er thy realms of waste but one small spot
Can speak to me or stir my soul:

A tiny rock, the glorious grave
And haunt of dreams of power lost,
Remembrance bare of fallen greatness,
Where raging pined Napoleon.

'T was there he died, slow torture's victim,
And now we mourn a loss as great:
For ever hushed the song of tempest,
That crowned him lord of soul of man.

He died bewept by freedom's children,
Bequeathing them his deathless crown.
Weep, ocean, weep, shed thy stormy tears!
His sweetest songs he sang to thee.

For on his brow was stamped thine image,
He, as it were, was child of thee;
Like thee, sublime, fathomless, alone;
Like thee, unconquered, unsubdued!

The world is dull and empty..... And now,
Whither, ocean, wouldst thou bring me?
Where'er man flies, his fate ne'er changes;
And should he sip the cup of joy,
Some tyrant's hand will dash it down.

Once more, farewell! And I thy beauty
And charms sublime shall ne'er forget;
And long, long shall, trembling, hear at night
The echo of thy mighty roar.

To forest shade, or the silent plain,
I ne'er shall bring a thought, save thine;
See thy cliffs, thy gleam, thy yawning gulfs,
And hear the chatter of thy waves.

ELEGY.

Beneath the deep-blue sky of her own native land,
    She weary grew, and, drooping, pined away:
She died and passed, and over me I oft-times feel
    Her youthful shadow fondly hovering;
And all the while a gaping chasm divides us both.
    In vain I would my aching grief awake:
From tongue indifferent I heard the fatal news,
    With ear indifferent I learned her death.
And yet, 'tis true, I loved her once with ardent soul,
    My heart of hearts enwrapt in her alone;
With all the tenderness of languor torturing,
    With all the racking pains of fond despair!
Where now my love, my pains? Alas, my barren soul
    For her, so light and easy of belief,
For memory of days that nothing can recall,
    To song or tears is dead and voiceless now.

VAIN GIFT, GIFT OF CHANCE.

Vain gift, vain gift of blindest chance,
    Life, why wert thou granted me?
Or why, by fate's supreme decree,
    Wert thou foredoomed to sorrow?

Alas, what god's unfriendly power
    Called me forth from nothingness,
My troubled soul with passion filled,
    Made my mind a prey to doubt?

An aimless future lies before,
    Dry my heart and void my mind,
My soul is dwarfed and crushed beneath
    Life's dull riot monotone.

—◦♦◦—

DROWNED.

The children ran up to the cot,
And eager to the father cried:
„Daddie, daddie, come quick, our nets
A body dead to shore have dragged!"
„You lie, you lie, you little imps!"
The angry father roughly growled:
„To think that these my children are!
I'll teach you talk about dead men."

Stern as judge, he 'gan to question;
„Alas, the truth I ne'er shall know,
There's nothing to be done! Eh, wife,
Give here my cloak, for I must go.
Where is this corpse?" „There, father, there!"
In truth, upon the river bank,
Where they the fishing-nets had cast,
A dead man lay upon the sand.

The corpse had lost its comely form,
All swollen now, of ghastly hue.
Some maddened wretch, who in despair
Had freed his erring soul from woe;
Some fisher caught in angry sea;
Some reeling royster homeward bound;
Or merchant rich, with well — filled purse,
Attacked by cunning thieves and robbed.

With this no peasant has concern!
He looks around, and sets to work;
With sleeves up-tucked, he quickly drags
To water's edge the sodden corpse;
And with his oar it pushes off
Adown the open, flowing stream;
And with the tide the dead man floats
In search of grave with cross o'erhead.

And long the body, tossed by waves,
Rolled, floating, like a living thing;
The peasant watched it out of sight,
And then he thoughtful home returned:
„Now, brats, to none a word of this,
And wastel-loaf I'll give to each;
But good heed take, and hold your tongues,
Or else a whipping you shall have!"

The night was rough, the storm-blast raged,
The river overflowed its banks;
Within the peasant's smoky hut
The flickering lath-torch spluttered;
The children slept, the housewife dozed,
And on his shelf the husband lay;

When, hark! above the tempest's howl
He heard some one at window knock.

„Who's there?".... Eh, open, my good friend
„Why, what ill luck is there abroad,
That thou, like Cain, dost prowl the night?
The devil take thee quick from hence!
For roaming vagrants where find place?
Our house is small and close enough."
And, with unwilling, lazy hand,
He window opened and looked out.

From out a cloud the moon peered forth...
Before him stood a naked form,
With water dripping from his beard;
His eyes were open, motionless;
A lifeless statue, numb and cold,
His bony hands drooped helpless down;
And o'er his swollen body crawled,
Fast clinging, black and slimy things.

The peasant quick the window closed;
He knew full well that naked guest,
And swooned away. „Ah, mayst thou burst!"
He, trembling, muttered trough his teeth.
Uncanny thoughts possessed his brain,
And all that night he sleepless tossed;
Till morn he heard the ceaseless knock,
At window first, and then at door.

Among the people goes the tale,
How from that night of dread and crime,

Each year the half-crazed peasant waits
The destined day and guest unknown.
From early morn the clouds hang low,
The night grows rough and wild with storm;
And lo! the dead man ceaseless knocks
At window first, and then at door.

THE UNWASHED.

A poet from enchanted lyre
Struck notes of mildest melody;
He sang.... but cold and all unmoved,
The mob unconsecrated stood,
And, gaping, listened to his song.

Amongst themselves the mob discussed:
„Why sing with voice so musical?
The ear is tickled, but in vain,
What is the goal he leads us to?
Why this thrumming? What would he teach?
Our hearts why stir, our souls torment,
Like one possessed with unknown tongue?
His song is free as lawless winds,
And, like the winds, can bear no fruit:
What good or profit can it bring?

POET.

Silence! mob of senseless grumblers,
Day-labourers, base slaves of slaves,
I loathe your shallow murmurs vile.

Ye worms of earth, no sons of heaven,
Your God is profit :..... by the pound
You weigh Apollo Belvedere:
The iron pot is dearer held,
Since it serves well to cook your food.

THE UNWASHED.

Nay, if thou be elect of God,
Thy gift, dear messenger divine,
Use kindly for our good and weal;
Correct and guide thy brethren's hearts.
We are, thou sayst, small-souled in aim,
Wicked, shameless, and ungrateful;
Our hearts are cold and dead to love,
Calumniators, slaves, and fools;
Each vice finds nest within our souls.
But thou art lover of thy kind,
And lessons bold in truth canst give;
And we will listen to thy words.

POET.

Away! Begone! What common tie
Can poet bind to such as you?
Be boldly hard in vice as rock;
Nor song, nor lyre can give you life,
In soul as senseless as the tomb;
For centuries you have well reaped,
And of your follies won the prize,
The whip, the prison, and the axe.
Begone, dull slaves of ease and gain!
Men in your city's noisy streets

The rubbish sweep.... a useful work!
But think ye that the prophet-priests,
Forgetful of their calling high,
Will quit the altar-sacrifice,
And meekly take in hands your brooms?
To take part in the world's turmoil,
In sordid gain, in vulgar strife,
We are not born, but have received
The inspired gift of sweetest song.

A WINTER MORNING.

The frost and sun; a glorious day!
And thou, my sweetling, still dost sleep:
'Tis time, my fairest, to awake:
Ope quick thine eyes with slumber dulled,
And gladly hail the Northern Morn,
Shine forth, thyself the Northern Star!

Last night the snow-storm whirled and roared,
The sky was hidden in white mist;
The yellow moon peered feebly through
The thick and gloomy flanks of cloud;
And thou satst dull and ill at ease,
But, darling, now.... look out abroad!

Beneath the richly woven web
Of dark-blue sky of deepest dye
The snow lies glittering in the sun;

The forest dense alone is black,
The firs are green with hoary rime,
And, bound in ice, the river gleams.

And all the room with amber glow
Is lighted up. The blazing fire
Up chimney flames with crackling gay,
'Tis good to muse in easy-chair:
But knowst thou what? 'Tis better far
To harness quick the chestnut mare.

And o'er the morning's snow our steed,
Full eager, with impatience hot,
Shall, panting, bear us, dearest, quick;
Across the empty fields we'll scud
Through thickest forests none could pass,
Along the shore so dear to me.

THE NOISY JOYS OF THOUGHTLESS YEARS ARE SPENT.

The noisy joys of thoughtless years are spent;
And all, like head confused with drink, is dulled.
But, as with wine, the woe of days gone by
With force more strong than newer woe torments.
A dreary path before me lies. Fresh toils
To drown me in a sea of trouble threat.

And yet, dear friends of youth, I would not die!
I wish to live, that I may muse and toil;

I feel that joy shall mingle with my woe,
Relieve my care, and heal my doubtings sad.
Once more, I'll drink the cup of harmony,
And drown my thoughts in flood of soothing tears;
And, haply, in the setting hour of life
Love's farewell smile 'shall lighten up the dark.

A STUDY.

And now, my chubby critic, fat burly cynic,
For ever mocking and deriding my sad muse,
Draw near, and take a seat, I pray, close beside me,
And let us come to terms with this accursèd spleen.
But why that frown? Is it so hard to leave our woes,
A moment to forget ourselves in joyous song?
And now, admire the view! That sorry row of huts;
Behind, a level long descent of blackish earth,
Above, one layer thick of gray, unbroken clouds.
But where the cornfields gay or where the shady woods?
And where the river? In the court there, by the fence,
Shoot up two lean and withered trees to glad the eye;
Just two, no more; and one of them, you will observe,
By autumn rains has long been bared of its last leaf;
The scanty leaves upon the other only wait
The first loud breeze, to fall and foul the pond below.
No other sign of life, no dog to watch the yard.
But stay, Ivan I see, and two old women near;
With head unbared, the coffin of his child he bears,
And from afar to drowsy sexton loudly shouts,

And bids him call the priest, and church-door to unlock:
„Look sharp! The brat we should have buried long ago!"

TO THE CALUMNIATORS OF RUSSIA.

What mean these angry cries, haranguers of the mob?
And wherefore hurl your curses at poor Russia's head?
And what has stirred your rage? Our Lietva's discontent?
Your wrangling cease, and let the Slavs arrange their feud:
It is an old domestic strife, the legacy
Of ages past, a quarrel you can ne'er decide.
    Already long among themselves
    These tribes have fought and weaved intrigues;
    And more than once, as fate has willed,
    We, or they, have bent before the storm.
    But who shall victor end the feud,
    The haughty Pole, or Russian true?
Shall streams Slavonic with Russian sea commingle,
    Or leave it dry? That is the question.
    Leave us in peace! You have not read
    These sacred oracles of blood;
    This fierce, domestic quarrel-feud
    Seems to you both strange and senseless!
    Kremlin, Praga, mean naught to you!
    You mock and scorn as childish whim
    The combat fierce we wage for life;

And more.... 'tis nothing new.... you hate us!
But why this hate? Nay, answer, why?
Is it because, when burning Moscow's ruins flamed,
We would not own his brutal rule,
Before whose nod you, humbled, crouched?
Because we rose and dashed to ground
The idol that so long had weighed the empires down,
And boldly with our blood redeemed
Lost Europe's honour, freedom, peace?

Your threats are loud; now, try and prove as loud in deed!
Think ye, the aged hero, sleeping in his bed,
No more has strength to wield the sword of Ismail?
Or that the word of Russian Tsar has weaker grown?
Or have we ne'er with Europe warred,
And lost the victor's cunning skill?
Or are we few? Erom shores of Perm to southern Tauris,
From Finnish cliffs of ice to fiery Colchis,
From Kremlin's battered battlements
As far as China's circling wall,
Not one shall fail his country's call!
Then send, assemblies of the West,
Your fiercest troops in full array!
In Russian plains we'll find them place
To sleep with those who fell before!

THE POET.

Prize not, poet, the vulgar love of people lewd;
The noise of popular applause will quickly pass,
The fool will give his verdict, and the mob will laugh;
But keep thou firm in soul, be tranquil and reserved.

Thou art a Tsar, must live alone! Along thy path
March freely as thy genius shall choose to lead;
And when thou hast brought forth the fruit of fancy free,
Seek not reward or praise for thy best achievements.

Thy sole reward is in thyself. Thou art thy judge:
And more severely than the rest will scan thy work;
Art thou content, creator stern and righteous?
Content? Then let the vermin mob condemn thy work,
Let them spit upon the altar where the fire burns,
And dash to ground in childish spite the tripod holy.

GOD GRANT, MY REASON NE'ER BETRAY ME.

God grant, my reason ne'er betray me;
Nay, better, fever-waste or want,
    Nay, better, toil and starve.

'Tis not that I my mind or wit
Have e'er prized high, or that with them
    I were not glad to part.

If but my freedom were untouched,
With joy and gladness would I make
    My home in forest dark.

With raving frenzy I should sing,
Myself forget, and lose my soul
    In weird discordant dreams.

Strength uncontrolled would then be mine,
Like wildest storm that sweeps the fields,
    And lays the forest bare.

Then I should hearken song of waves,
Be filled with joy, and gaze upon
    The empty, vacant sky.

Ay, there's the rub: to lose my mind,
Be feared, as men do fear the plague,
    And close in prison locked:

And when the madman's chained, in crowds
They'll come, and through the grating stare,
    And tease the surly beast.

And then, at night, compelled to hear,
Instead of nightingale's high note,
    Or forest's murmur soft,

The frantic shrieks of prison-mates,
Muttered oaths of warders sullen,
    And creaking noise of chains.

MY MONUMENT.

I've reared myself a monument not made with
    hands;
The path to it shall ne'er be overgrown with grass,
Where it with high, unbending head shall tower
    Above Napoleon's column.

Not wholly shall I die: the soul that nursed my
    muse
My dust shall long outlive and shall defy decay;
And men shall love to chant my lays, whilst on our
    earth
    A single bard doth breathe or sing.

My fame shall live and be a Russian household
    word,
And all who speak our tongue my name shall whis-
    per soft,
The Slav of ancient race, the Finn, the wild Tungese,
    And Calmuck born on barren steppe.

And long shall I the people's favourite be held,
Since ne'er my lyre has failed to stir all feelings pure;
My verse the general cause has singly pleaded,
    And pity for the fallen taught.

To God's high will, my muse, in lowly meekness
    bow;
Let no rebuff offend, nor laurel crown demand;
Take praise or calumny with like indifference;
    And never argue with the fool.

THE GIPSIES.

A POEM.

THE GIPSIES.

I.

In noisy crowds the gipsies bold
Their way through Bessarabia tramp;
To-day they pitch their camp and set
Their tattered tents by river-side.
As free as bird, they choose their haunt,
And peaceful sleep 'neath open sky.
From midst the wheels of waggon-vans,
Half-covered with thick canvas roofs,
Curls high the flame, and round the fire
Within their tent the family group
Prepare with care the evening meal.
In open field the horses graze;
Beyond the tent the tamed bear lies;
And all is gay along the steppe
With busy cares of household life,
With women's songs, and children's laugh,
And measured beat of blacksmith's stroke,
As they prepare for morrow's march.
And now, o'er all the nomad camp
Unbroken silence calmly reigns,

And naught is heard on tranquil steppe,
Save bark of hound or neighing steed.
Throughout the camp the fires are quenched,
And all is peace. The moon, sole queen
In heaven's expanse, sheds forth her rays,
And bathes the sleeping camp in light.
All sleep, save one old man who sits
Before the half-extinguished fire
And warms himself with its last heat.
And oft he scans the fields remote,
Enwrapt in evening's soft, white mist.
His daughter young and fair is wont
In all to have her way, and now
Has gone to stroll the lonely fields.
She will come back; but it is late,
And o'er the moon the clouds of night
Already gather thick and fast.
But no Zemphire returns: meanwhile,
The old man's modest meal grows cold.

    At last she comes, and close behind
Follows along her path a youth,
A stranger to the gipsy sire.
„See, father mine", the maiden said,
„I bring a guest; beyond the mounds
I found him lost on the wild steppe,
And refuge in our camp I offered.
He lies beneath the ban of law,
But I have sworn to be his friend;
Aleko is his name, and he,
Where'er I go, will follow me."

OLD MAN.

I welcome thee. Remain the night
Beneath the shelter of our tent;
Or, if thou wilt, stay longer here,
As thou thinkst fit, for I consent
Our board and roof with thee to share.
Be one of us, and learn our fate
To bear, the fate of vagrants poor,
But free, and with the early dawn
Shalt find a place with us in van,
And prove what trade art skilled to ply:
The iron forge.... or sing a song,
And show the villagers our bear.

ALEKO.

I will remain.

ZEMPHIRE.

He shall be mine:
And who shall chase him from my side?
But it grows late; the crescent moon
Has set; the fields drink in the mist;
And heavy sleep weighs down mine eyes.

II.

'Tis dawn. Around the sleepy tent
With watchful steps the old man strolls.
„Arise, Zemphire, the sun is up;
Awake, my guest, 'tis time to march:

Quick, children, quit the couch of ease!"
With busy haste they all start up;
The tents are raised; the waggon-vans
Stand ready for the long day's march.
At given sign the swarming crowds
Begin to make their slow descent
Through steep defiles precipitous.
In hand tilt-carts the asses draw
Their close-packed loads of children gay;
And mingling groups of old and young
In orderly disorder move.
Loud cries, and shouts, and gipsy songs;
The bear's low growl, and frequent creak
Of his impatient, irksome chain;
The particoloured, tattered robes;
Shoeless men half-clad and children;
The angry bark and howl of dogs;
The noisy bagpipe's piercing notes;
The grating harsh of turning wheels:
A picture wild and dissonant,
But all alert and full of soul;
Unlike our world's benumbing ease,
Unlike the barren life of town,
A life as dull as chant of slaves.

III.

With weary glance the youth looks back
Upon the now unpeopled plain;
Nor can he yet the secret cause
Of grief that fills his heart discern.

Beside him lies the black-eyed maid;
Lord of himself, lives as he will;
And o'er him shines the glowing sun
In his rounded midday beauty.
What, then, torments his youthful soul?
What care disturbs his restless heart?

    The bird of air is free and knows
Nor anxious toil nor daily care;
Nor fretsome seeks to weave a nest,
That shall defy the ages' wear;
But on the branch the long night sleeps,
Till sun shall don his morning robe,
And then, responsive to God's call,
With quickened thrill sings out his song.
When spring, fair nature's darling child,
Gives place to sultry summer's heat,
And later autumn brings its due,
Dark clouds, and mists, and frequent rains,
Men's hopes fall low, and they are drear;
The bird to other distant lands,
To warmer shores and bluer seas,
Will fly, and wait return of spring.

    Like the bird that is <u>free from care</u>,
An exile lone, bird of passage,
He knew not where to lay his head,
Nor was there aught to touch his soul.
To him the world lay open wide,
Nor cared he where he strayed or slept;
But each new day he freely left
To fate's disposal and control.

The changes and alarms of life'
Thus failed to break his peace of mind.
At times, the far-off star of fame
Would tempt him leave his ease, and climb;
In vain, the world before him spread
Its idle pomps and pleasures vile;
Not seldom o'er his lonely head
The thunder roared and threat'ning broke;
But naught he recked of tempests rude,
And dozed alike in storm and calm;
He lived his life, nor recognised
The power of blind and cunning fate.
But, God! what passions wild have stormed
Aleko's seeming tranquil breast!
With what mad fury have they raged,
And torn in twain his wounded soul!
And thinks he to have tamed them now?
They shall awake, their hour will come!

IV.

ZEMPHIRE.

But say, my friend, dost not regret
The world thou hast behind thee left?

ALEKO.

And what is there to leave?

ZEMPHIRE.

                Thou knowst:
Country, friends and native city.

ALEKO.

Wherefore regret? Ah, didst thou know,
Couldst but once conceive or measure
The vileness of their stifling town!
Where men do herd in crowds, nor breathe
The morning fresh, or mountain free,
Or scent of spring on meadow sweet;
Are shamed of love, and banish thought,
Consent to sell their freedom dear,
To fetish idols bow their heads,
Will sue for pelf, and hug their chains.
What have I left? The falser's lie,
The smirking bigot's narrow creed,
The senseless hate of unwashed mob,
Rank, orders, title, bought with shame.

ZEMPHIRE.

But there are mansions vast and rich,
There are carpets varicoloured,
There are balls and banquets gayest,
And there are jewelled maidens fair.

ALEKO.

What gain can bring the town's mad joys?
Where love reigns not, joy cannot be.
Better far than all their maidens,
Art thou, Zemphire, though poorly clad,
Of jewels and of necklace bare!
Change not, my true and faithful friend,
And I'll keep true to my sole wish,

With thee will share my love, my cares,
My life, in willing banishment.

OLD MAN.

I see, thou lovst us and our folk,
Though born amidst a people rich;
But freedom is not always dear
To him who has been born in ease.
Amongst us runs a legend old:
From southern climes was banished once
A stranger to our land.... his name
I knew, but have forgotten since....
He was already old in years,
But still was young in heart and soul;
Possessed the wondrous gift of song,
And voice like murmur of the waves.
And all who knew him loved him well,
And on the Danube's shore he lived,
Offended none, and none despised,
Enchanting all with song divine;
Was not proud, nor reasoned wisely,
But weak and timid, like a child.
For him our folk would hunt the beast,
Or trap the fish in close-knit net;
And when the river swift would freeze,
And wintry winds began to howl,
For him, their aged favourite,
They deftly stitched warm skins of fur.
For he was strange to petty toil
And all the tasks of daily life,
And lived a wand'rer pale and poor.

An angry god had punished him,
He said, for some offence and crime.
And now he prayed that death might come;
And as he roamed the Danube shore,
His grief he shared with its blue waves,
And oft would shed hot, burning tears,
At thought of his far-distant home.
And ere he died, he prayed that we
His body to the south would bring;
For never could he sleep in peace,
Unless in his dear earth he lay,
His home once more his native land.

ALEKO.

Such fate awaits thy noblest sons,
Oh Rome, great empress of the world!
Singer of love, hymner of gods,
Tell me, what is poet's glory?
A grave unknown, obscure; the theme
Of legend passed from mouth to mouth;
The nameless hero of wild tale
By gipsy told in smoky tent.

V.

Two years have passed, and as before,
The peaceful band of gipsies free
Are ne'er refused, but easy find
A friendly welcome and repose.
All social lies and cheats thrown off,
Aleko is as free as they;

Regretting naught and spared all care,
Their roaming life he daily shares.
He is the same, nor have they changed;
The years gone by he has forgot,
And gipsy life is now his own.
The tent's hard couch on which he sleeps,
Unconscious of the morrow's fate;
The routine march of ease unbroke;
The language poor, but soft and sweet;
In all he finds alike delight.
The bear, its native haunt forgot,
Is now the sharer of his tent.
In villages that skirt the road,
They stop before Moldavian homes;
To please a timid, gaping crowd,
The bear will dance his clumsy step,
And grol wimpatient at his chain;
And, leaning on his pilgrim-staff,
The old man idly beats his drum;
Aleko, singing, leads the bear;
Zemphire is sent to make the round,
And beg from each a small reward
But night has set, and they all three
The evening meal prepare to share.
The old man sleeps and all is still;
Within the tent dead silence reigns.

VI.

The tents gleam bright in spring sun's rays,
The old man warms his sluggish blood,
His daughter sings a song of love,
Aleko listens and grows pale.

ZEMPHIRE *(singing)*.

 Husband old, husband fierce,
Burn, hack me with thy sword'
I am bold, do not fear
Either sword or <u>fire's flame.</u>

 Knowst thou not, I hate thee?
Knowst thou not, I scorn thee?
Another has my love,
And, loving, I can die!

ALEKO.

 Cease, I pray, thy singing wearies,
Nor do I like such savage rhymes.

ZEMPHIRE.

 My song offends? But what care I?
'Tis for myself alone I sing.

 Burn, hack me with thy sword,
No word shalt hear from me;
Husband old, husband fierce,
His name I'll ne'er betray!

 He's fresher than the spring,
He breathes warm summer's heat
With daring youth he glows,
And none but me he loves!

 Softly I caressed him
In shadow of the night,
As merrily we laughed,
And mocked at thy gray hairs!

ALEKO.

Cease, Zemphire, cease! It is enough!

ZEMPHIRE.

And hast thou understood my song?

ALEKO.

Zemphire!

ZEMPHIRE.

    Be angry, if thou wilt:
It was to thee I sang my song.
          (*She goes away singing*).

OLD MAN.

  I remember, I remember,
It is a song of olden days;
And years ago, to please our folk,
Marie would sing this rhyme to them.
On winter nights, when we were camped
On the Kagoula barren steppes,
Marie would chant the savage lay,
And rock the child before the fire.
I lose all count of byegone days,
And quickly fades their memory;
But this one song has ta'en deep root,
And still I hear its mocking notes.

VII.

Now all is still; 'tis night; the moon
With silver tips the southern pole.
Sudden the gipsy-sire is roused
From sleep by Zemphire's touch and voice.

ZEMPHIRE.

In his sleep Aleko frights me;
He tosses, groans, and sighs, and weeps.

OLD MAN.

Disturb him not, but silence keep.
I oft have heard the Russians say,
At night, the demon of the house
Will haunt the troubled sleeper's dream,
And then at dawn itself depart.
Till then, 'tis well thou sitst by me.

ZEMPHIRE.

In sleep he starts, and cries, Zemphire!

OLD MAN.

Though dreaming, still he seeks for thee:
Dearer than all thou art to him.

ZEMPHIRE.

And yet, his love has brought no joy:
My heart would fain throw off the yoke,
Be free again.... But hush!... listen!
He mutters now another's name.

OLD MAN.

Whose name?

ZEMPHIRE.

       Dost thou not hear? He groans,
And grinds his teeth. 'Tis horrible!
I will awake him quick.

OLD MAN.

                Why seek
To chase the demon of the night?
It will itself depart.

ZEMPHIRE.

                 I hear
Him restless turn, and now he calls:
I go. Farewell! Sleep, father, sleep!

ALEKO.

Where hast thou been?

ZEMPHIRE.

             I was with father.
Some evil spirit did torment
And plague thee in thy sleep. I dared
No longer stay. But thou didst grind
Thy teeth, and called me.

ALEKO.

             In my dream
It seemed as if between us was....
But no! it is too horrible!

ZEMPHIRE.

Dost thou believe in cheating dreams?

ALEKO.

In none, in naught, do I believe;
Nor dreams, nor lover's secret vows;
Nor that thy heart can loyal keep.

VIII.

OLD MAN.

And why, in vain caprice of youth,
Dost thou, like furnace sighing, moan?
Here men are free, the skies are bright,
And women own no fetter-bonds.
Grieve not, nor be cast down in soul.

ALEKO.

But, father, she no longer loves.

OLD MAN.

Console thyself: she is a child.
Thy grief to reason is perverse:
Thou lovst with passion and with fire;
A passing jest is woman's love.
Look up; beneath the wide expanse
The moon pursues her unchecked path,
And, as she moves, she gently sheds
Her fickle light on all below;
A moment gilds a favoured cloud,

Only the next to leave it dark,
And flood its rival with her light.
But who shall stop her trackless course,
Bid her stay and no farther roam?
And who shall say to maiden's heart,
Love one, and only one, ne'er change.
It cannot be.

ALEKO.

How she loved me!
How tenderly she bent o'er me,
And in the silence of the night,
Her head soft pillowed on my breast,
With childish mirth and innocence
Whispered, laughing, tender nothings,
And with caresses winsome could
In one short moment chase away
All gloomy thoughts and craven fears!
And now, thou tellst me, she is false,
That she, Zemphire, no longer loves!

OLD MAN.

Hearken, and I will story tell
Of myself and years long, long past,
Before Moscow had tried to win
Her new domains on Danube shore.
You see, I would recall, my friend,
The sorrow of far, younger years.
The mighty Sultan then we feared;
The Pascha ruled the Budschack plain,
And lofty heights of Ackermann.

Then I was young, and my glad soul
Within me leaped, all free of care;
And then my jet-black, raven curls
Flowed down unmixed with elder gray.
Among the maidens young was one,
Their queen in beauty.... long I loved
And worshipped her, as men the sun;
At last I won her.... she was mine!
Alas, like falling star, my youth,
Gleaming, flashed, and quickly vanished:
But swifter far the reign of love
Rose and flitted by; ....one short year,
And Marie, my queen, betrayed me!
Near the wide, deep lakes of Kagoul,
We chanced to meet a stranger tribe,
Who pitched their tents at mountain's foot,
Where we had made our sojourn brief;
Two nights we friendly camped together,
And on the third they sudden left.
With them.... her daughter left behind,
Marie escaped to pleasures new.
I sleeping was, and when dawn broke,
And I arose, I found her not!
I called.... in vain.... no answer came!
Many a day poor Zemphire pined,
And wept; my tears I joined with hers.
But from that day my heart grew cold,
Unstirred by maiden's wiles or charms;
Nor have I sought a mate to share
My lot; but all alone have passed,
Resigned, the cheating hours of life.

ALEKO.

And wherefore didst thou not at once
Pursue the faithless perjured pair,
And plunge thy dagger in the heart
Of robber and his paramour?

OLD MAN.

But why? Youth is free, free as bird.
Who has strength to curb the flight of love?
To each one day of joy is sent;
And what has been can ne'er return.

ALEKO.

Mine not the nature to forego
My right without a struggle fierce,
Be robbed the joy of sweet revenge.
Nay, if on brink of ocean cliff
I found my hated foe asleep,
I swear, I should not think to spare
His life, but with my foot would toss
O'er edge of cliff his helpless trunk,
And laugh in his pale, upturned face
Of wakened horror and surprise.
And in mine ear the water's splash
Would echo like the stirring sound
Of conquering march loud and gay.

IX.

YOUNG GIPSY.

Yet one more kiss, before we part!

ZEMPHIRE.

Time flies: jealous he is, and harsh.

YOUNG GIPSY.

A last.... but long caress.... but one!

ZEMPHIRE.

Farewell, before he comes to seek me.

YOUNG GIPSY.

But say, when shall we meet again?

ZEMPHIRE.

To-night, when as the moon goes down,
We'll meet beyond the mounds. Farewell!

YOUNG GIPSY.

You will forget to come, I fear.

ZEMPHIRE.

Away!... Fear not!... I'll come, I swear!

X.

Aleko sleeps. But dreams confused
Disturb and haunt his troubled rest;
And with a startled cry he wakes,
And stretches forth his jealous hand,
Which falls on cold and vacant sheet;
No sleeping Zemphire lies by him.

With boding heart he listens long,
But all is still; and, filled with dread,
A chilling fear runs through his veins,
As out he hurries from the tent.
Pale and trembling, far he wanders,
But all the field is wrapt in sleep
The moon is hid behind the clouds,
And twinkling light of stars is dim.
The faintest track of steps, the dews
Have nigh effaced, still show the way
That leads up to the burial mounds.
With eager pace he makes his way,
By demon urged along the path,
And stands before the long-ranged heaps,
That rear their pale and spectral tops.
And, filled with sense of coming ill,
Scarce his aching limbs can bear him:
With quivering lips and trembling knees
He pushes on.... and does he dream?
He sees two shadows close to him,
And hears the murmured whisper near,
That floats above the lonely mounds.

FIRST VOICE.

'Tis time!

SECOND VOICE.

Why this haste?

FIRST VOICE.

I must away!

SECOND VOICE.

Nay, rather let us wait the day!

FIRST VOICE.

'Tis late!

SECOND VOICE.

How timid is thy love!
One minute!

FIRST VOICE.

Wilt thou be my death?

SECOND VOICE.

One minute more!

FIRST VOICE.

But if he wakes,
And finds me gone?

ALEKO.

I have awaked!
Whither so fast? There is no haste!
'Tis well, we need not search for graves!

ZEMPHIRE.

Darling, run, escape!

ALEKO.

Stay, sir, stay!
Whither, fair gipsy, wilt thou run?
Die!
 (*He kills him with a dagger.*)

ZEMPHIRE.

What hast thou done?

YOUNG GIPSY.

I die! Farewell!

ZEMPHIRE.

Aleko, thou hast slain my friend!
And, see, thou art all stained with <u>blood!</u>
Oh, what hast thou done?

ALEKO.

I? Nothing!
His love, once thy breath, breathe it now!

ZEMPHIRE.

Enough! I have no fear of thee!
Thine empty threats, I hold in scorn!
Thee and thy bloody crime, I curse!

ALEKO.

Follow!
(He stabs Zemphire).

ZEMPHIRE.

And, loving, I will die!

XI.

Night's clouds were streaked with red of dawn.
Beyond the hills Aleko sate
Alone on ancient burial mound,
With blood-stained dagger in his hand.
Near him lay two lifeless bodies;
His face was fixed and motionless,
And vacant stared at gipsy crowd,
Who fearsome stood around and gazed.
In farther field they dug a grave;
With solemn step the women moved,
And kissed the eyelids of the dead.
Apart the old man stood and looked,
In silent helplessness of grief,
Upon the dead girl's rigid form.
Lightly they raised the bodies twain,
And slowly bore them to the grave,
And laid the youthful erring pair
In the cold bosom of the earth.
Aleko from afar watched all,
But when the last handful of dust
Over the sleeping dead was cast,
In silence low he bent his head,
And prone on grass fell from the mound.

The old man then approached and said:
„Go, leave us now, thou haughty man!
We wild folk have no law to bind,
To torture, or to punish men;
We need no sinner's blood, or groans,
Nor can we with a murd'rer live.

Thou art not born for wild free will,
Thou wouldst thyself alone be free;
Thy voice will strike but terror here
Among the good and free in soul;
Harsh thou art and rash: so, leave us!
Farewell, and peace abide with thee!"

He spake, and now the busy crowd
The nomad camp begin to raise:
They hasten forth, and soon are lost
To view. One van alone, with roof
Of canvas torn, remains behind,
And stands upon the fatal field.
As when, before cold winter comes,
At early hour, on misty morn,
A flock of cranes will from the field
Rise up on high with eager cry,
And quick begin their southern flight,
One wretched bird, the sportsman's prey,
With wounded wing that helpless hangs,
Is left behind to pine and die.
Though night came on, within the van
None cared to kindle light or fire,
And none beneath the tattered roof
Sought rest or sleep till morning broke.

EPILOGUE.

The magic charm of song divine
Brings back to life the olden days,
Writes anew on memory's page
The record of past joys and griefs.

In the land where centuries long
The din of war not once was hushed;
Where Russian arms supremely marked
The lawful bounds of Stamboul's sway;
And where the mighty eagle shook
His proud, wide wings o'er triumphs won;
'Twas there, the wild steppe stretching round,
On borders of our ancient rule,
I met the gipsy waggon-vans,
The sons of freedom uncontrolled.
I long in idle whim pursued
Through barren waste and forest wild
The gay and lawless gipsy band.
Their modest, simple fare I shared,
And slept before their flaming fires.
I loved the noise of their loud songs.
And still the name of fair Marie
Haunts and startles my restless sleep.

And yet, with you, free nature's sons,
True happiness can ne'er be found;
And humblest tents are oft the haunt
Of troubled dreams and hopes destroyed;
And nomad camps, though pitched in wilds,
From nature ravin give no shield;
There, too, will human passions rage,
And naught protect men from their fate.

POLTAVA.

A POEM IN THREE CANTOS.

POLTAVA.

CANTO THE FIRST.

Rich and famed is Kotzubei.
Boundless and large his spacious fields,
Whereon his droves of horses graze
At their free will and all unwatched.
Around Poltava's fairest plains
Stretch far his gardens and his parks;
And in his house are treasures rare
Satins, furs and dishes silver,
Exposed to view or safely locked.
But Kotzubei, rich and proud,
Cares little for his long-maned steeds,
The tribute paid by Tartar horde,
Or lands bequeathed him by his sires;
But in Marie, his daughter fair,
The old man finds his dearest pride.

In vain you'll seek Poltava through
Her peer in loveliness and grace.
Fresh as primal flower of spring,
Warm-nurtured in the forest's shade;
As Kieff poplar tall and stately;

Her every motion like the course
Of floating swan on lonely lake,
Or deer's quick flight across the mead;
Her breasts as white as foam of sea;
Around her forehead high and broad,
Thick clustered lie her jet-black locks,
Veiling her eyes that gleam like stars;
Her lips as red as full-blown rose.
But not the charm of beauty rare,
That blooms a moment and then fades,
Had made Marie beloved by all;
But fame had crowned her with the name
Of maiden modest, pure and wise.
And rival suitors sought her hand,
The youths of Russia and Ukraine;
But from the marriage-crown, as from
The fetters of a slave she shrank.
And all had been repulsed.... but now
His messengers the Hetman sends.

No longer young, and worn with years,
With toils of war and cares of state,
But young and warm in heart, once more
Mazeppa feels the force of love.

A boyish love will fiercely burn,
Its fierceness spent, as quickly die;
The passion cools, to be renewed,
And finds each day some fancy fresh.
An old man's heart disdains to burn
With such obedient, lightsome ease,
The victim of a moment's whim:

But dulled and dimmed with thoughtful years,
The fire of passion tempered flames;
The heart is proof against its force,
And slow to burn; but once 'tis stirred,
The love born late can ne'er grow cold,
And only dies with parting breath.

It is no deer that seeks a refuge sure,
Alarmed by eagle's heavy flight;
It is a bride her chamber roams,
And, trembling, waits her parents' word.

All filled with angry discontent,
The mother comes, as one distraught,
Seizes her hand, and sharply cries:
„Now, shame befall the godless wretch!
Can such things be? No, whilst we live,
He ne'er shall wreak his foul desire!
Well fit to play the father, or
The friend to god-child young and pure,
The senseless fool, in dotage years,
Forsooth would ape the husband's part!"
Naught spake Marie. But o'er her face
A creeping pallor slowly flushed;
And cold and stiff, like lifeless corpse,
Prone on the floor the maiden fell.

She woke to life, and then once more
Her eyes were closed, nor did she speak
One single word. With busy care,
They seek to ease and cheer her soul,
To drive away her fears and grief,

To peace bring back her unhinged mind;
But all in vain. For two whole days,
Now weeping sad, now choked with sobs,
She neither spake, nor eat, nor drank,
But pale and sleepless, like a ghost
Compelled to walk, she knew no rest.
The third morn they went to seek her,
But found her chamber bare and lone.

None knew, or when, or how, Marie
Had fled. That night, a fisher said,
He heard the tramp of swiftest steeds,
The Cossack speech, and woman's voice;
Next morn the marks of eight horse-hoofs
Were traced along the dew-wet mead.

'Tis not alone the first soft down,
The curling, wavy locks of youth,
But oft the look serene of age,
The deep-streaked brow, and snowy hairs,
That win a maiden's fancy free,
And light her soul with dreams of love.

Too soon the hateful tale of shame
Assailed the ear of Kotzubei:
She had forgot disgrace and fame,
To wanton in a wretch's arms!
Nor he nor wife dared comprehend
The whispered hints of common talk.
Ere long the story was confirmed,
Made true in all its vilest shame.
Only then was bared the secret

That long had stained the maiden's soul:
Only then they learned and understood
Why wilfully she had rebelled
Against the curb of married life,
And, lonely grieving, pined away;
Or why the love of noble youths
Had been repulsed with silent scorn;
Or why at table Hetman's speech
She would drink in with greedy ear,
And when the noisy chat grew gay,
And foaming goblets flowed with wine,
And she was asked to sing, she chose
No songs save those himself had made,
When he was young, unknown to fame;
Or why, with passion strange to maid,
She loved to watch the rangèd troops,
And hear the kettledrum and shouts
That hailed the golden staff and mace,
The Hetman's signs of rule and sway.

Lordly and rich is Kotzubei,
Has hosts of friends to serve his will;
Can wash away in blood this shame,
And rouse Poltava to revolt;
With sudden blow his palace storm,
And wreak a father's vengeance deep;
With sure and fatal aim can pierce....
With other thoughts his soul is stirred.

The times were ripe with troubled broil:
In threatened struggles hard and stern
The young empire must try her strength

And slowly reach her full manhood
Beneath great Peter's rule. Meanwhile,
A chast'ner cruel had been sent
To teach her how to win her fame,
And more than once the Swedish King
Had sharp and bloody lesson taught.
But, trained in durance and hard toil,
She bore the harshest blows of fate,
And grew. For thus, the hammer stout
The glass will break and forge the sword.

With glory crowned that bore no fruit,
The Swedish Charles essayed his fate.
'Gainst Moscow's ancient walls he marched,
And chased the bravest Russian troops,
As whirlwind drives the valley's dust,
And low bends down the highest grass.
The route he followed was the same
By which, in later days, the lord
Of fate pursued his hurried flight.

Ukraine was mined with discontent,
And long the spark had smouldered dull.
The children of the stormy past
Nursed hope to fan a people's war;
With murmurs grim they clamoured loud
That Hetman burst their slavish chains;
And with the zeal of untried youth
Impatiently awaited Charles.
Around the aged Mazeppa rose
The rebel cry: „To arms! to arms!"
But true the Hetman old remained,

The slave and vassal of the Tsar.
He ruled as sternly as before,
And in the Ukraine guarded peace:
Seemed blind to all that passed around,
And lived and feasted at his ease.

„What is this Hetman?" snarled the young.
„He is too old, he is too weak.
Unresting years and toil have quenched
The youthful fire that once flamed bright.
With trembling hands does he presume
To wield the lordly staff and mace?
Now is the time to wage the war
On hated Moscow, freedom's foe.
If Doroschenko, aged in years,
Or young Samoilovitch, the exile,
Palaeus brave, or Gordienko,
Now ruled the warriors of Ukraine,
Cossacks would ne'er be left to die
In snow-wastes of a distant land;
Our troops no more would be compelled
To serve the cause of foreign rule."

Thus murmuring, the self-willed youths
The dangers of revolt would court,
Forgot their country's thraldom long,
Forgot Bogdan's successful rule,
The treaties, and the sacred war,
And all the fame of ancient times.
But old men walk with heedful care,
And calculate with cautious mind
What they should do, and what forbear,

Nor will they thoughtlessly decide.
What man can sound the depth of sea
Fast bound with massive thick-set ice?
Who hope with keenest eye to pierce
The cave profound of cunning heart,
Whose thoughts are fruit of passion crushed,
And hidden lie from common view,
Whilst secretly some cherished dream,
Perchance, is ripening all unseen?
Such none can know. The Hetman false
Was most deceitful, cunning, sly,
The simpler, more sincere, he seemed,
The franker and more true in act.
He knew the art to read, to win,
To tyrannise the souls of men;
And, whilst he seemed himself to yield,
To rule their minds and guide their thoughts.
With what false faith and simpleness
Like garrulous old man, he talked
With those who were his peers in age,
Regretting happy, olden times!
With self-willed youths he freedom preached;
With discontents he darkly spake;
Shed tears of pity with the wronged;
With fools was wise and deeply grave.
A few, it may be, knew full well
That none could tame his iron will;
That he, by foul or honest blow,
Would surely thwart and crush his foe;
That never to his dying day
He pardoned or forgot a wrong;
That love of power heartless stretched

His crime-stained deeds and selfish schemes;
That naught was sacred in his eyes;
That kindness could ne'er touch his heart;
That ties of love were weak to bind;
That blood he freely shed unmoved;
That liberty he scoffed and scorned;
And that he knew no fatherland.

Long the traitor, false and cunning,
Had planned and mused a deadly plot;
But sharper, keener eyes than his,
Those of a foe, his scheme had bared.

„Nay, base kite, breeder foul of shame!"
The old man cried and gnashed his teeth,
„Thou needst not fear, I'll spare thy home,
My wretched daughter's prison-house;
Thou shalt not perish in its flames,
Nor find release in easy death
From Cossack blow. Not so, vile one!
In the hands of Moscow headsman,
In vain denials of thy guilt,
In torture, writhing on the rack,
Thou shalt curse the day, curse the hour,
When thou wert sponsor to our child;
The banquet when I filled to thee,
And loving-cup of honour drank;
The night when, like a bird of prey,
Thou durst to steal our darling dove".

There was a time Mazeppa old
And Kotzubei were close friends;

When ties of friendship bound them fast
With household bread, and salt, and oil;
When oft their steeds, close side by side,
Had brought them safe through scudding shot;
When oft, in secret room secure,
The Hetman would a part reveal
Of his unsated, restless heart;
Would darkly hint in careful phrase
Of coming change, and treaties new,
And well-planned popular revolt.
Of this he spake, for in those days
The father of Marie was pledged
To aid and help Mazeppa's cause.
But now, the slave of passion fierce,
He had alone one aim in life:
Himself be slain, or else to slay,
His child dishonoured to revenge.

Meanwhile, his bold and daring scheme
He keeps close hidden from the world.
„I'm old and powerless", he said,
„I have one wish, the grave's sweet sleep.
The Hetman will I work no harm,
My daughter was alone to blame;
A father's blessing I will give.
Let her to heaven the crime atone,
That brought dishonour to our house,
And shamed the law of God and man".

He now, with eagle glance full keen,
Among his house-retainers seeks
A faithful, trusty servant bold,

Resolved in will, and incorrupt;
Confides his purpose to his wife:
And, filled with more than woman's spite,
The wife, all bent to strike the blow,
Will nothing hear of wise delay,
But, in the silent waste of night,
Like spirit restless and untombed,
Quick vengeance whispers in his ear,
And, with reproachful tears, entreats
Him swear to sweep to his revenge;
Until he binds himself by oath.

   The blow is planned. With Kotzubei
The bold Iskra in concert acts.
And both believe: „We must succeed,
Our hated foe shall surely fall.
But where's the man, whose eager zeal,
Devoted to his country's weal,
Will tempt him brave the Hetman's rage,
And dare to lay at Peter's feet
The damning proofs of his false guilt?"

   Among the Cossacks of the Don,
Whose suit the maiden had repulsed,
Was one who from his youngest years
Had loved her with the purest love.
At morn, or in the evening hour,
Along his native river's shore,
Beneath the Ukraine-cherry's shade,
He oft would-wait the fair Marie,
And, waiting, pined, till one soft word
Should healing bring to his sad heart.

He knew too well, he loved in vain,
Nor ever urged a useless prayer,
Lest loss of her should make the world
A void. And when his comrades gay
Proclaimed their noisy vows of love,
He silence kept, nor spake a word.
But now her name is linked with shame,
And gossip, glad to scoff the fallen,
Makes her the theme of unclean wit,
Marie still keeps her early rights,
And is to him what she had been.
And if, perchance, Mazeppa's name.
Were in his presence praised or blamed,
His face grew pale, and, lost in grief,
He sat with eyes cast down to earth.

Who rides his steed so fast and late,
With naught to guide him save the stars?
Whose steed scuds o'er the boundless steppe,
With straining neck and loosened girth?

The Cossack keeps the northern tract,
Nor will the Cossack slacken pace
In open field, or forest grove,
Or check his steed near dang'rous ford.

Like crystal clear his sword shines bright,
A bag is girded to his breast;
Nor stumbles once his mettled steed,
But gallops on with flowing mane.

The rider needs his well-filled purse,
The soldier's pride is in his sword,

The restive steed is his dear pet;
But dearer still is his fur cap.

Sooner than it, he well might lose
His steed, full purse, and shining sword;
Would fight to death in its defence,
And shed last drop of his wild blood.

What makes his cap so dear to him?
Within it lies the missive hid,
Wherein the Hetman is denounced
As traitor to the mighty Tsar.

Unconscious of the brooding storm,
And fearing naught from secret foe,
Mazeppa weaves his subtle plot.
The jesuit, his close ally,
Excites the people to revolt,
And gives him promise of the throne.
The two, like thieves, at night debate
The sum that buys each man they need;
Invent a cipher safe and sure,
That none their treason may suspect;
They fix a price on Peter's head;
With cheating oaths their vassals bribe.
An almsman... none knew whence he came...
Begins to haunt the palace-folk;
Orlick, the rebel Hetman's aid,
Oft sends him there, or calls him thence; —
Where'er they come, his purchased spies
Disorder spread and discontent.
They raise the Cossacks of the Don,

Ally themselves with Bolavine,
The wild horde's love of war enflame,
And far beyond the Dnieper-falls
Sow fears of Peter's iron rule.

None scape Mazeppa's watchful eye;
From north to south, from east to west,
Both far and wide he missives sends.
By cunning threats Crimean Khans
Are set to war against Moscow.
The King of Poland follows suit;
And Turkey lends her ready hand;
Whilst Charles prepares to draw the sword.
Active, alert, he knows no rest,
Awaits the hour to strike the blow;
Nor does his will one moment slack,
As he pursues his guilty aim.

Like thunderbolt from clearest sky,
The crushing blow Mazeppa dazed;
But not for long: new plots are schemed.
He soon received from Russian lords,
Despatched to him, their country's foe,
The missive from Poltava writ,
In place of blame, caressing words,
As if he were base slander's prey!
And, plunged in troubled cares of war,
The Tsar condoled with Judas false,
And, angered, took the false for true,
The warning words unheeded left;
Resolved ere long to crush revolt
By punishment severe and stern.

With feignèd grief he sends the Tsar
His cringing plea of loyal faith:
„God and man I call to witness,
For twenty years your willing slave
Has served his Tsar with truth and zeal;
And far beyond his meed enjoyed
His master's gracious love and trust.
But spite is ever rash and blind!
What gain if, in declining years,
He learns to play the traitor's part,
And blast with shame his unstained name?
Was it not he with righteous scorn
Refused to aid sly Stanislas,
Refused the proffered Ukraine crown,
And, moved by duty's call, disclosed
The lying traitor's papers false?
Was it not he, by Khans approached,
Renounced alliance with the Turk?
Was it not he proved well his zeal
Against the White Tsar's banded foes,
And step by step, with brain and sword,
Thwarted their plots, and freely risked
His life to win his liege's cause?
And now they dare dishonour bring
Upon his hairs in service gray!
And who? Iskra and Kotzubei,
Who both so long had been his friends".
And, coldly shedding poisoned tears,
Triumphant in his insolence,
The wretch demands their instant death.

Whose death? Oh, man of iron will,

Whose daughter, nestling, warms thy breast?
The sleepy whisper of remorse
Is hushed by heartless reason cold,
And thus he dulls the still, small voice:
„The stubborn fool hath freely sought
The fight unequal and foredoomed;
With hoodwinked eyes he courts defeat,
And gives the axe a keener edge.
Where can he fly with eyes close-shut?
What hope can fan his proud conceit?
Or thinks he... No! the daughter's love
Shall ne'er outbuy the father's life.
The lover to the Hetman yields,
Or else, disgraced my blood must flow!"

Alas, Marie! What fate betides thee,
Marie, Circassia's peerles bride?
Knowst thou not what deadly serpent
Now feeds and fattens on thy breast?
By what unknown, mysterious power
Art thou with strongest fetters bound,
Tied to a harsh, corrupted heart?
To whom art thou a docile slave?
His flowing locks of silvered hair,
His searching eyes, deep-set and keen,
His brow well scathed with lines of thought,
His music voice that knows to charm,
To thee were dearer than world's wealth;
For them thou couldst forget and dare
A father's wrath, a mother's love;
For them prefer a couch of shame
To home's sweet care and shelter sure.

His wondrous eyes that pierce the soul
Have cast on thee their witching spell;
His pleading vows of reckless love
Have lulled the warning voice within.
As on the face of worshipped saint,
Thou lookst on him with blinded gaze,
Repaying love with love more sweet.
As others find in virtue joy,
Thy very shame thou makst thy pride,
And in thy fall hast ever lost
The priceless charm of woman's shame.

    She heeds not shame nor scorn of men:
What now to her the world's repute?
The proud old man oft bends his head,
And lowly lays it on her knee;
Forgets with her the plaguing toil,
The noise and cares of outer world;
Reveals to her, the timid maid,
His hopes and fears, his wily schemes.
But, though she ne'er regrets the past,
At times, a thick and labouring cloud
Creeps o'er and darkens all her soul.
Before her rise the griefful forms
Of father stern and mother pale;
With dimming eyes she sees them there,
Abandoned in their childless age,
And thinks to hear their soft reproach.
Ah, if but now she only knew
The common talk of the Ukraine!
Alas, from her is closely kept
The secret of revenge and crime.

CANTO THE SECOND.

In gloom Mazeppa sits. His mind
Is tossed with fear of failure's shame.
Marie, with wistful eyes of love,
In silence watches her old man,
Approaching softly, clasps his knee,
And sweet words whispers in his ear.
In vain: no more her love has strength
To chase away his musings dark.
Cold he lowers his absent glance
Before the kneeling maid, nor deigns
Reply to her reproaching look.
Stung to the soul, in wonder lost,
Half choked, she rises from her knees.
„Listen, Hetman", she cries, „for thee
I have forgotten home and all.
And when my soul chose thee her lord,
I had but one desire... thy love:
For that I sacrificed my all!
Nor do I now regret the past.
Rememb'rest thou how in that night,
The night I gave myself to thee,
To love me ever thou didst swear:
Tell me, then, why thy love has ceased.

MAZEPPA.

Hearken, Marie, thou art unjust.
Shake off these vain and childish fears!
Let not doubt sow poison in thy heart,
Or blinded passion idly stir
And vex thy young and ardent soul.
Believe, Marie, my love for thee
Exceeds my love of rule or fame.

MARIE.

'Tis false, and thou dost play with me!
Then were we one in heart and soul;
My fond embrace thou fleest now,
My love has dull and irksome grown.
Thy days are with the elders spent,
At feasts or raid,... and I alone!
All night, close locked in room, thou art
In counsel with the almsman-priest.
If I renewal seek of love,
My sole reward is cold repulse.
And yestern eve, I learn, thou drankst
To Dulskaya... 'twas news to me...
Who is this Dulskaya?

MAZEPPA.

And art
Thou jealous, then? Is it for me,
Already aged and worn in years,
To seek from heartless courtesan
A greeting cold, or passing smile?
Shall I, the stern old man, begin

To play the skipping youngster's part,
And, sighing, lustful sport in chains,
To win a wanton's idle glance?

MARIE.

Nay, answer me without deceit,
And answer simply: yes or no.

MAZEPPA.

To me thy peace is ever dear.
Thy will be done, and learn the truth.
With caution have we hatched the plot,
That now is ripe for quick success.
Propitious are the times; the hour
Has come to strike the fatal blow.
Deprived of freedom, robbed of fame,
Too long we bear a foreign yoke,
Now as Warsaw's humble vassals,
Now slaves to Moscow's tyrant rule.
In freedom's cause the sword we'll draw,
Nor fear I 'gainst the Tsar himself
The standard of revolt to raise.
Our plans are formed; allies are found;
And secret treaties have been drawn
Between myself and both the kings;
And soon, as fruit of battle fierce,
May be, a royal throne I'll rear.
Friends I have, whom I can trust,
Princess Dulskaya, Zalenskoi,
Together with the almsman sure;
And they will bring my scheme to end.
'Tis through their faithful hands the kings

Their orders and instructions send.
And now thou knowst our dread designs,
Art thou content? And are thy doubts
Now laid to rest?

    MARIE.

    Oh, dearest chuck!
Thou shalt be our new country's Tsar!
And well the royal crown shall suit
Thy snowy locks!

    MAZEPPA.

    Stay, soft awhile!
As yet it is not won. The storm
But lours. Who knows what fate will bring?

    MARIE.

 Where thou art, fear can have no place.
Thou art so mighty! Well I know,
The throne awaits thee!

    MAZEPPA.

    Or the block!

    MARIE.

 If so, with thee I share the block
Dost thou think, I will survive thee?
But no! thou wearst the kingly sign.

    MAZEPPA.

Lovst thou me, Marie?

MARIE.

I? Love thee?

MAZEPPA.

But tell me, which, sire or husband
Dost thou the dearer hold?

MARIE.

Nay, friend,
And why this question? Or why delight
To torture me in vain? My home
I would forget. To them I am
A thing of shame! And who can know?...
Oh, thought to make the boldest blench!...
May be, my father has accursed me,
And for whom?

MAZEPPA.

But am I dearer
Than father? Silent still?

MARIE.

Ah, God

MAZEPPA.

Well, answer me!

MARIE.

Reply thyself!

MAZEPPA.

Suppose, thou must pronounce the word,
Which of us, thy sire or I, should die?

Whom wouldst thou doom to condign fate,
Whom wouldst thou save from sentenced death?

MARIE.

Oh! cease! Tear not my heart in twain!
Why play the tempter's part?

MAZEPPA.

Reply!

MARIE.

Thou art all pale; thy speech is harsh;
Look not so fierce! All, all, I am
Prepared to give. Believe, I lie not;
Though thus to speak is still a crime!
Enough!

MAZEPPA.

Remember well, Marie,
The words thou hast so freely spoke.

Calm and soft is the Ukraine night.
No cloud to dull the wide expanse;
The stars are shining full and bright;
No breeze to wake the drowsy dream,
Nor scarce a breath that cares to fret
The sleep of silver-poplar leaves.
On town and Hetman's gardens gay,
And on the hoary castle-tower
The moon her tranquil light unveils.
And all around is hushed and still,
But all within is noise and haste;
Near lattice window in the tower,

Deep sunk in grief and gloomy thought,
Sits Kotzubei, bound in chains,
Watching the peaceful sky above.

To-morrow morn he's doomed to die.
For him the scaffold has no dread,
And life has naught he need regret;
Nor fears he death, the wished-for sleep,
The sleep that rests the worried flesh.
But, righteous God! to be thus gagged,
And crushed beneath a villain's feet,
Like some brute beast to slaughter led!
The Tsar to make him Hetman's game,
That he, false traitor to the Tsar,
May boast and triumph in his fall!
To lose his life, and with it fame!
To bring his friend to shame and death,
And hear him, guiltless, curse his name!
To meet his foe's triumphant look,
As when he lays his head on block!
Be thrown into the arms of death,
Ere he bequeath to kinsman sure
The sacred task of vengeance keen!

Poltava dear in dream he sees;
Its wonted group of household friends,
The happy days of wealth and ease,
The songs his daughter loved to sing,
The ancient home where he was born,
The friendly scene of all his joys,
Where he had known hard toil and sleep,
And all that he had cast away,
For what?

In rusty lock is heard
The grating key, and, roused from dreams,
The wretched captive thinks: 'Tis he,
My guide, along the path of blood,
To hold up high the cross divine,
Tho bearer of the keys of heaven,
The healer of the wounded soul,
The minister serene of Christ,
Who suffered death and ransomed us;
The sacred gifts immaculate
He brings, that, strengthened and confirmed,
I may the bolder march to death,
Nor fail to reach immortal bliss.

With softened heart old Kotzubei
Before the Ruler of the world
Prepares to pour his heart in prayer;
But 'tis no gentle anchorite
Has come with words of pardon free:
The hated Orlick stands before him.
And o'er his face a loathing comes,
As he demands with proudful scorn:
„What wilt thou here, oh man of crime?
What moves Mazeppa to disturb
The last remains of my sad life?"

ORLICK.

One secret more thou must divulge.

KOTZUBEI.

I have replied: and so, depart,
Leave me in peace!

ORLICK.

                One answer more
Our lord demands.

KOTZUBEI.

                       And what demand?
I have revealed, acknowledged all
That thou wouldst know. The charges made
Were all a lie. I'm skilled and sly
In weaving plots. The Hetman's right.
What more canst thou require?

ORLICK.

                            We know,
Riches thou hadst and stores untold;
These stores in slily chosen spots,
In thy village of Dianka,
Thou hast concealed and hidden kept.
This wealth, in forfeit of thy crime,
Is due to Cossack's common fund.
Such is the law. That law obey.
No more delay, but tell us quick
Where are the treasures thou hast hid?

KOTZUBEI.

    Well, thou art right! Three treasures were
The pride and joy of my whole life.
The first of these my honour was,
And this the rack hath robbed me of.
The second none can give me back,
The unstained name of daughter dear,
That day and night I, tending, watched;

Mazeppa hath that name defouled.
The third and last I guard mine own,
My third and last is... vengeance just;
And that I take with me to God!

ORLICK.

Cease, old man, these idle ravings!
Think, on verge of life thou standest,
Proud defiance ill befits thee,
No time to trifle. Answer give,
Or else thou feelst the torture sharp!
Thy moneys, where?

KOTZUBEI.

Recreant slave!
Cease, I pray, thy questionings vain.
And when I lie within my grave,
Then go, thy lord Mazeppa seek,
And with grim fingers steeped in blood
Count o'er my treasures and my wealth,
Break ope my unprotected vaults,
My plundered home with fire destroy!
Methinks, 'twere well to take Marie,
She will my secrets all betray,
And show you where each treasure lies.
Do what thou wilt, but in God's name
Leave me, and let me die in peace!

ORLIK.

Thy moneys, where are they? Say, quick!
Thou wilt not speak? Thy moneys, where?
Or bitter shall thy tortures be!

Think well, the hidden wealth disclose!
Say, where; or rack shall make thee tell!
Once more, speak, or else... What ho, there!

The headsman crossed the cell.

       This night,
Where is the Hetman? What does he?
How sting of conscience hope to still?
In the chamber of the happy maid,
Blest in her ignorance of ill,
Beside his sleeping godchild's couch,
Mazeppa sits with head bent low,
A prey to care that gives no rest.
Dark thoughts flit chasing through his mind,
Still darker than the thoughts they chase.
„This self-willed, dotard fool must die!
The hour of our success draws near,
And stern must be the Hetman's power
Wherewith he should invest himself;
Remorseless must the Hetman crush
Who would oppose. Without appeal
The bold informer and his tool
Must die!" By hap, he casts his glance
On Marie's couch. „Oh God! and what
Will be with her when first she learns
The sentence dread has been fulfilled?
As yet her soul is undisturbed,
But it no longer can be kept
From her. The headsman's fatal blow
Like thunder-stroke will echo loud
Throughout the whole Ukraine. The talk

Of prating world will reach her ears.
Alas, I see, the man, ordained
By fate to lead the world's big strife,
Alone should face the raging storm,
Unhampered by a woman's love.
The restive steed and timid deer
Must ne'er be harnessed to one car.
This I incautiously forgot,
And now must pay the heavy price
Of my mad fault. For, all that has
Worth, all that lends to life a charm,
The blameless maiden brought to me,
To me, a stern old man... and I,
In what can I reward her love?"
Fondly he gazes where she lies,
Cradled and stilled in softest dream.
How sweet her sleep of trusting faith!
A happy smile her lips half part,
With fullest life her white breasts heave!
But to-morrow?... And with a groan
He rose, and, with quick muffled steps,
Reeled blindly forth into the air.

Calm and soft is the Ukraine night.
No cloud to dull the wide expanse:
The stars are shining full and bright;
No breeze to wake the drowsy dream,
Nor scarce a breath that cares to fret
The sleep of silver-poplar leaves.
Mazeppa's soul is filled with strange
Conflicting thoughts. The stars of night
Look down like keen accusing eyes,

And haunt him with their mocking glance.
The poplars hug their branches close,
And shake their tops, and whisper low
To list'ning boughs their sentence stern.
The balmy air of summer night
Chokes him, like damp of prison cell.

Sudden, as from the castle near,
He hears a cry... a speechless moan.
Is it the coinage of mad brain,
The owlet's hoot, or wild beast's growl,
Or tortured groan? He cannot tell.
But he is powerless, the slave
Of some strong will, and in reply
Shouts back the wail... his fierce, loud cry
He raised when in the battle's din,
With Zabel, or with Hamelei,
Or oft with him,... with Kotzubei,
He rushed to meet the foe's wild charge.

The first faint streaks of russet dawn
Have bathed the sky in new-born light;
The vales, and hills, and meadows gleam;
The tufted groves and rippling streams
Awake to sing their morning hymn,
And summon men to daily toil.

Still lying on her couch, Marie
In slumber dozing, thinks she hears
In her light sleep some one approach,
And touch her foot with timid hand.
She wakes, but quickly with a smile

Her eyes are closed, as from the glare
Of day they shrink. And in her sleep
She stretches and puts out her hand,
As languidly she murmurs low,
„Mazeppa!" But a voice, not his,
Replies, and, trembling, she looks up,
And what is it she gazes on?
Before her stands her mother.

                MOTHER.
                            Hush!
Or else we are undone! This night
I've hither stolen, and am come
With one, last, sad, beseeching prayer.
To-day he dies. And thou alone
Canst touch or turn their cruel hearts.
Thy father save!

                MARIE.
                    Whose father save?
Who dies?

                MOTHER.
                    Or can it be, till now
Thou hast been ignorant?... But no!
Thou livst with him, art in the world,
Must know how dread the Hetman's sway,
How all his foes before him fall,
And how the Tsar puts trust in him..
I see too well, thy ruined home
Thou hast forgot for Hetman's love!
The sentence dread hath been pronounced,

The death-decree is being read,
The axe is raised above his head,
And thou art sleeping at thy ease!
I see, we are but strangers now.
Marie, arise, run, kiss his feet,
Our angel be, thy father save!
One look from thee will stay the wretch,
And turn aside the falling axe.
Be earnest, urgent in thy prayers!
Thinkst thou the Hetman will refuse?
It is for him thou hast renounced
The claims of honour, home, and God!

MARIE.

Alas, what do I see and hear?
Mazeppa... father... death... and here
My mother, praying, kneels before me!...
Nay, nay, my fancy plays me false,
I must be mad!

MOTHER.

God be with thee!
'Tis neither madness nor a dream!
It cannot be, thou dost not know;
Thy father, wounded in his pride,
Unused to bear a daughter's shame,
And thirsting quick and sharp revenge,
Betrayed the Hetman to the Tsar.
Knowst thou not that, racked with pain,
He hath accused himself of false
Intrigues 'gainst innocence and truth?
That he, the prey of justice blind,

Lies at the mercy of his foe?
This day, before the Cossack troops,
Unless just God should intervene,
He dies the death of public shame.
Within this castle's prison-tower
Bound and chained he lies.

MARIE.

                Oh God! oh God!
'Tis true?... this day... my father dies?

  And on her couch the maid down drooped,
And backward fell, like some cold corpse.

  The gay caps mingle in the sun;
The spears shine bright; the drums beat loud;
The Hetman's well-trained troops march forth
To take their rank in ordered file.
With throbbing hearts the crowds swarm round.
The road, that winds like serpent's tail,
Is filled with teeming, surging throngs.
Aloft in square the scaffold glooms,
And on its boards the headsman struts,
Rubbing his hands, his victim awaits;
As 'twere a toy, from time to time,
Plays with his heavy sharp-edged axe,
Or with the mob exchanges jest.
A noise confused is heard around
Of laughter, railing, murmurs, cries.
A sudden shout is raised, and all
Are hushed, and through the silence deep
Is heard the tramp of horses' hoofs.

By body-guards surrounded close,
The Hetman on his rampant steed,
With gay and gallant suite, appears.
Along the road to Kieff straight
Slow trails a cart. All eyes are turned,
And eager watch its slow approach.
Within it sits old Kotzubei,
At peace with God and erring man,
Full strong in faith that makes men bold.
Resigned and pale sits Iskra near,
Like lamb that is led forth to die.
The cart draws up. The full-voiced quire
With hymn of prayer the calm air fills.
Thick clouds of incense mount on high,
As silent all, with head uncovered,
Pray for those condemned to die.
And they about to suffer pray
Their foes may pardoned be, and, slow
Descending, climb the fatal steps.
With sign of cross and prayer for all
He leaves behind, the old man lays
His snow-white head upon the block.
A silence dead creeps o'er the crowd;
The axe is raised; a moment's flash,
And severed falls the head below:
A smothered groan the silence breaks.
With gruesome thud a second falls,
And stains the thirsty grass with blood.
Proud of his work, the headsman grim,
Seizing the still wet tufts of hair,
With arm all bared and far outstretched,
Dangles the heads before the mob.

And all is done. The fickle crowds
Break up, and to their homes disperse;
In groups discuss among themselves
The petty cares of daily life;
And soon the square is emptied quite.
Along the road with gay crowds covered,
Two women quickly push their way.
Foot-sore, thick stained with clinging dust,
Possessed with fear, they hurry on,
Eager to reach the fated spot.
„You are too late", a peasant cries,
And points with finger to the place,
Where now half-torn the scaffold yawns.
Robed in black a priest is praying,
And two Cossacks have piled a truck
With coffins made of roughest oak.

Alone, Mazeppa, grim and stern,
Aloof from his bold troopers rides.
An unfilled void torments his heart,
And earth and heaven alike are dull.
Not one so rash to dare come near,
Not one who cares a word exchange.
All in foam his black steed bears him,
And, reaching home, Marie he calls.
His serfs are summoned. In reply,
Unmeaning words they stammer forth.
Against his will a prey to fear,
He hastens to her room, but finds
The maiden's chamber lone and bare.
Madly he roams the garden's length,
Searches each bush and beats each brake,

Around the lake each crevice pries:
But all in vain; no trace he finds.
And now he calls his troopers sure,
Picked men who long have served him well;
They hurry forth on panting steeds,
The wild chase-cry resounds afar,
As here and there the brave youths rush,
Nor leave a hidden nook unsearched.

A hundred roads are quickly scoured:
But no Marie, alas, returns!
No one has known, and none can tell,
The secret of her hurried flight.
In silent rage Mazeppa grieves;
His vassals shrink from him in fear;
His poisoned breast within him burns;
And closely locked he bars his room,
And, staring at the vacant couch,
Speechless he sits the whole night long,
Stung with pains that are not of this world.
Next morn, the slaves he had despatched
Return, their errand unfulfilled.
Their tired steeds can scarcely move. Girths,
Bridle and hoofs, and housings gay,
Are drenched in foam, or stained with blood,
Broken, or lost upon the road.
But none has brought his master stern
Of maiden news. No trace they found,
And she, it seemed, had disappeared,
As though the world had ne'er known her.
The mother fled her house of woe,
And begged her bread from stranger hands.

CANTO THE THIRD.

Though plunged in griefs that are his own,
Not less the ruler of Ukraine
His bold and daring scheme pursues.
True to his plans he stands resolved,
And with the Swedish King concludes
A secret pact against the Tsar.
Meanwhile, the better to deceive
The watchful eyes of hostile spies,
Some leeches wise he quickly calls,
As on the bed of sickness feigned
He groans and whines for instant help.
The passions, toils and cares of war,
The woes and weakness of old age,
Death's harbingers, have laid him low.
But he, no more the dupe of life,
The passing world is glad to leave.
Religion's rites he would observe,
And bids his trusty priest to come,
And on his hoary locks is poured
The healing oil of balm and peace.

But time goes by. In vain Moscow
The threatened guests each hour awaits,

And midst the graves of her old foes
For Swedish slain prepares a place.
A sudden change of march is made,
And Swedish troops invade Ukraine.

    The day has come, and from his bed
Mazeppa rose, this suff'rer weak,
This living corpse, who yesternight
The last, sad rites demurely served.
But now, the rival of the Tsar
To Desna hotly makes his way,
With ardent eyes before his troops
His sword high waves and boldly rides.
All signs of age he now throws off,
Erect, and strong, and young, appears,
Like prelate who, in years well struck,
Is called to wear the Papal crown.
The wingèd news spreads far and wide:
„The Hetman false has humbly laid
At feet of Charles his golden mace."
The fire quick catches, and the flames
Of civil war burst forth.

                    But who
Shall tell the Tsar's fierce rage and wrath?
The churches echo ban and curse;
The hangman burns Mazeppa's bust;
In noisy council's hot debate
Another chief the Cossacks choose;
And from their place of exile far
The kin of Iskra and his chief
Are summoned back. With them the Tsar

Bewails their sires' unrighteous fate,
And subtly whets them to revenge.
And old Palaeus, horseman bold,
His youth renewed, once more returns,
The camp to join and fight the foe.
The Ataman, the bold Tchetchel,
Is seized and cast in dungeon deep.
And thou, who threwst away a crown
For warrior's helm, thy fated day
Is near; Poltava's ancient walls
At last thou seest from afar.

And now, the Tsar his troops has massed,
Wave after wave succeeding fast,
And in the centre of the vale
The two opposing camps are pitched.
Not once in skirmish bold repulsed,
From early years made drunk with blood,
With all a warrior's joy Charles sees
At length the wished-for day arrive,
When he and his dread foe, the Tsar,
In battle face to face shall meet.
He has his wish, but finds himself
Confronted with no runaways,
As when he fought at Narva, but
With soldiers well accoutred, brave,
Obedient, and self possessed,
With sure and trusty weapons armed.

„To-morrow morn we battle give!"
He thus resolved; and all was still
Throughout the camp, save where two friends
Together whispered converse held.

MAZEPPA.

Nay, Orlick, I too late perceive
What unwise rashness we have shown;
Bold was our scheme, but badly planned;
Nor can we hope achieve our end,
But rather failure and disgrace.
Our error naught can now redeem.
This Swedish King I have mistook;
A stripling rash who with success,
Of course, can two, three battles wage,
And from the field will straightway ride
And sup at Dresden with the foe;
Will with a jest defiance take;
Or, like some common Russian scout,
Prowl leaguered camp at night, and come
On Cossacks sitting round the fire,
And shot for shot with them exchange.
But strife to wage with Russian Tsar
Is not reserved for such as he.
Like troops, he would manoeuvre fate
And make it march to sound of drum.
Self-willed he is, impatient, blind,
Light-minded, and a braggart rare;
Puts trust in what he calls his star;
Against new forces of the foe
Can only pit successes past,
And so will get his wings close clipt.
It shames me that in my old age
I have been gulled by this war-crow,
Been blinded by his airs, seduced
By his good luck and future hope,
As though I were some ninny lass.

ORLICK.

'Tis wiser wait the fight's result;
The fitting moment has not come
With Peter friendship to renew:
Our error yet we can repair.
From victor's hand, there is no doubt,
The Tsar will terms of peace accept.

MAZEPPA.

Nay, 'tis too late: the Russian Tsar
And I can ne'er be friends again.
My fate was long ago foredoomed,
From ancient times our feud begins.
At Azoff once, the whole night long,
In royal tent the savage Tsar
Kept noisy feast. The goblets, filled
With sparkling wine, went gaily round,
In suit with freest jest and speech.
Some ill-considered word I spoke;
The younger guests looked on with awe;
The Tsar grew hot with wrath, down dashed
His cup, and seized me by the beard,
And swore to vent his sov'reign rage.
My fruitless anger I subdued,
But in my heart I vowed revenge.
As warm her child a mother keeps
Within her womb, that vow I nursed.
The hour has struck. Till his last day,
Of me remembrance will he keep.
To him I am an eyesore keen,
A canker in his crown's fresh leaves.

His herited domains, his life's
Best, dearest hour he would forego,
Once more Mazeppa by the beard
To hold. But let us not lose hope.
The morn decides who victor proves.

   He ceased, and soon the traitor false
Closed fast his heavy eyes in sleep.

   The russet sky is streaked with dawn.
Along the vales, along the hills,
The rumbling cannons raise thick clouds
Of dust, that high ascend and dim
The first, faint rays of early morn.
The troops close up in serried ranks;
Bayonets cold are shouldered fast;
Out-skirmishers take up their post;
And bullets speed, and shots whiz by.
The favoured sons of mighty war,
The Swedes, break through the trenches' fire;
The eager horsemen push their way;
Behind them march the men on foot;
Whose firm, unbroken columns give
Support to each bold, forward move.
The field of battle dubious
Is now the scene of noisy din;
And fickle fortune turns her wheel,
And on our arms her first smile throws.
Their troops before our fire retreat,
And in confusion fall away.
Now, Rosen through the defile flees,
And Schliepenbach, the rash, submits.

We press the Swedes from post to post,
The glory of their flag now wanes;
The Lord of Hosts protects our cause
And crowns our arms with full success.

'Twas then was heard, as from on high,
A mighty voice, that thundered loud:
„On, children, on, and God with us!"
Surrounded by his heroes leal,
He sallies forth. His eyes gleam fierce;
His face is stern, and terror strikes.
Quickly he moves. His noble form,
Dark-louring like God's thunder-storm,
Destruction breathes. The steed is brought,
And restive, but submissive, stands;
Scenting afar the smoke and fire,
It trembling darts its eyes askance,
And proudly bears its rider bold,
Who seemed to know his fiery steed.
Beneath the burning midday sun
Awhile the raging battle slacks,
Though Cossacks still keep up the fire.
But now the troops are drawn in line,
The trumpet, flute, and drum are hushed,
From hills no longer cannon flash
Across the plain their hungry roar;
And far around the welkin rings
With deaf'ning shouts and loud hurrah,
The soldiers' welcome to their Tsar.

Before his troops he quickly moves
In all his might and martial pride,

As with keen glance the field he scours.
Behind him ride, in compact crowd,
The boast and glory of his age,
In all the changes of blind fate,
In all the toils of rule and war,
His fellow-workmen and his mates:
Brave Scheremeteff, honour's theme,
And Bruss, and Bauer, and Repnine,
And Menschikoff, kind fortune's child.
The prop and pillar of the realm.

Meanwhile, before the rangèd ranks
Of his best troops and heroes brave,
In litter borne by faithful slaves,
Pale in face and motionless,
With bandaged arm, King Charles appears.
Around him crowd his brilliant suite.
Deep plunged in thought, his troubled face
Is marked with signs of anxious care:
As though the combat he desired
Was now a thing of fear and doubt.
——And, like a man compelled by fate,
He feebly waves his tired hand,
Begins the fight he long had planned,
And moves his troops against the foe.

Our men across the smoking plain
March quick to front the fierce assault,
The shock of great Poltava's day!
Amidst a shower of red-shot hail,
That strikes and breaks the wall of flesh.
Each time a rank falls out, fresh rank
Supplies its place, and heavy clouds

Of horsemen, scudding to the sound
Of clattering arms, in maddened fray,
Around them deal fast blows of death.
The fiery balls fly here and there,
And, spreading death, heap pile on pile
Of heroes slain, or soil dig up,
Or hissing fall in streams of blood.
The mingled foes strike, hew, and wound:
And naught is heard save beat of drum,
The roar of cannon, cries of rage,
The heavy tramp, and dying groan;
And death and hell hold feast unchecked.

 Amidst the terror and dismay,
Unmoved the leaders calmly watch
The progress of the doubtful fight,
Pursue the tactics of their troops,
Foresee the ruin and the conquest,
And oft in whispers converse hold.
But who may be the warrior gray
That near the Moscow Tsar close stands?
By two Cossacks held up, his heart
Once more with youthful zeal burns fierce,
As with the soldier's practised eye
He views the busy scene around.
Grown old and weak in exile long,
No longer can he leap on steed;
No longer will Palaeus see
At his brief summons Cossacks haste.
But wherefore flash his eyes so keen,
And with dark rage, as with night-mist,
His agèd face is mantled deep?

What passion is it moves him thus?
Or does he through the battle smoke
Mazeppa spy, and at the sight
His years decrepit vainly curse?
Mazeppa, thoughtful and disturbed,
Surveys the field, as round him press
A crowd of mutinous Cossacks,
Kinsmen, elders, body-troopers.
A sudden shot! The old man turned.
In Voinarovsky's close-clenched hand
The barrel of his gun still smoked.
A few steps made, the young Cossack
With bleeding wound from saddle rolled.
The steed, all bathed in foam and dust,
Scenting freedom, wildly snorted,
And soon was lost in thickest smoke.
On Hetman rushed the Cossack fierce
Across the field, with sword in hand,
His eyes afire with madman's rage.
The old man met his eager foe,
And would a question put. But ere
He could reply, the brave Cossack
Had breathed his last. His glazèd eyes
Still bore the glance of hate, and seemed
To seek revenge on Russia's foe.
One instant ere he closed his eyes,
His face grew bright with sudden gleam,
As with a sigh he softly lisped
The name „Marie", and, smiling, died.

Each moment nears the happy hour;
Our men push on, the Swedes retire;

We charge, and they disrouted flee;
Headlong pursuit our horsemen give.
The swords grow blunt with slaughter's work,
The plain is covered thick with dead,
As with a swarm of locusts black.

There is high feast in Peter's tent:
Right proud and keen, and bright his glance.
And all within is joy and pomp,
As, to his troopers' noisy shouts,
He welcomes one and all his guests,
Pays honour to the captive Swedes
In goblets crowned with nine salutes,
His teachers in the art of war.

But where the first and honoured guest,
Our chiefest teacher and most feared,
Whose rage and long nursed hate this day
The victor of Poltava stilled?
And where Mazeppa, Judas false,
Has refuge found and fled in fright?
Among the guests where is the King,
Or why has block the traitor spared?

The ill-starred mates of common flight,
The King and Hetman, breathless urge
Their steeds across the barren steppe.
The dread of shame and danger near
Inspire the King with novel force;
No more he cares for aching wound.
With head bent low, he hurries on,
Outstrips with ease the swift pursuit,

And gallops fierce, that of his men
But few have strength to keep the pace.

Abreast with him the Hetman rides,
And anxious is the glance that scans
The wide expanse that stretches far:
Before them lies a farmstead bared.
Why grows Mazeppa pale with fear?
Why hurries he, as panic-struck,
And, spurring steed, fast dashes by?
Or does the sight of yard and home,
And garden waste, and open gate
That leads into the field, awake
Within his heart an aching dream
Of wrongful deed and crime most foul?
And does the ravisher once more
Behold that cloistered shrine,
That home, the scene of mirth and joy,
Where he, his heart unlocked with wine,
Surrounded by the household gay,
And welcome guest, was wont with jest
At midday feast to gladden all?
Is this the house, the refuge sure,
Where once the angel unstained dwelt?
Is this the garden, whence that night
The maiden pure he lured across
The steppe?... Too well he knew the place!

The shades of night fall o'er the plains
Along the Dnieper's grassy shore;
Among the rocks they lightly sleep,
The foes of Russia and her Tsar.

The hero's sleep is lulled with dreams,
And he forgets Poltava's shame.
But broken is Mazeppa's sleep,
His gloomy soul finds no repose,
And in the silence of the night
His name is whispered. Starting up,
With frightened gaze he looks around,
And, trembling as beneath the fall
Of sharpened axe, before him sees
A silent form, with finger raised.
And there, with loose, dishevelled hair,
With bright and glittering, sunken eyes,
In garments torn, full pale and wan,
A moon-ray falling on her, stands...
„Or do I dream?... Marie!... 'Tis thou?"

MARIE.

Hush, hush, my darling! But just now,
Have father, mother, closed their eyes:
So, wait... or they may hear us... hush!

MAZEPPA.

Marie, ah poor Marie, I pray,
Recall thy thoughts! What dost thou here?

MARIE.

Listen the trick they have dared play,
The juggling trick they have devised!
Last night she came with warning words
That father had been done to death,
And secretly an old white head

She showed to me. Oh, righteous God!
Where can we fly from man's deceit?
For, think, the head she brought with her
Bore not the shape of human skull,
Was like a wolf's... You see, the kind
She is! With cheating lies like these
She thought to trick and gull her child:
Now, shame on her to torture me!
And why? That I might courage lack
With thee, my love, this night to flee:
Can people be so base?

      In dread,
Her lover looks on her wild face:
But she, distempered fancy's slave,
Quick whispers: „I remember all,
The field... the folk in dresses gay...
The crowd... the bodies warm, but dead...
I went with her to see the show...
But where wert thou?... And why, alone,
Apart from thee, at night, I fled?
But let us quick return, 'tis late!...
But ah! My head is ill, my brain
Is racked with empty, idle dreams:
Strange! I took thee for another...
Nay, nay, I pray thee, touch me not!
Thy glare is cruel, cold as ice,
And ugly! But he was beautiful:
His eyes were soft with kindest love,
His words were fair and gracious,
His beard was whiter than the snow:
But thine is clotted with dry blood!"

And with a shriek of laughter mad,
And swifter than the hunted deer,
She wildly burst his hold, ran forth,
And in the silent waste was lost.

The last thin shades of night disperse,
The east begins to redden bright;
In Cossack tents the fires burn clear,
And busy hands the meal prepare.
Along the banks the body guards
The steeds unbridled lead to drink,
And Charles awakes. „'Tis time!" he cries,
„Arise, Mazeppa, dawn is near!"
But long the Hetman has not slept;
His heart is drear, the choking grief
Mounts high, his breath comes thick and hard;
Silent he sets the saddle right,
And he and Charles pursue their flight.
At last they cross the border-point;
The Hetman's eyes are dimmed with tears,
As home and country fade from view.

MOZART AND SAGLIERI.

A DRAMATIC SKETCH IN TWO SCENES.

MOZART AND SAGLIERI.

SCENE THE FIRST.

A Room.

SAGLIERI.

Men say, there is no justice on this earth.
And above, there is no justice either!
This is as plain and clear as simplest scale.
The love innate of art divine is mine;
And whilst a child, whene'er in our old church
The organ swelled in high and thrilling notes,
I hearkened and drank in the sounds, till tears,
Self-moved but none less sweet, flowed down my
                                                      cheeks.
From earliest years all pleasures I forswore;
In studies strange to music found no charm;
From them with proud contempt I kept aloof,
And music vowed with all my soul to serve.
The trial step was hard, and dull the path
I had to tread. My primal failures soon
I overcame. The simpler handicraft
I made to serve as stepping-stone of art;

Became the common workman; taught my hand
A sure and firm, but pliant, flowing touch,
And gained a nice and precise ear. I slew
The sounds, and, like a corpse, dissected them.
And when I knew all science had to teach,
Would have of art creative brightest dreams;
Myself began compose, but secretly,
Nor ventured yet to think of glory.
Nay oft, when in my silent cell alone,
Some three days long, unheeding sleep or food,
I had the glow of inspiration felt,
The rapture past, I burned my work, and watched
The notes that were an echo of my soul
Upshrivel fast, and vanish in light smoke.
Nay, what say I? When the great master, Gluck,
Appeared to us revealing secrets new,
Secrets divine, profound and ravishing,
Renounced I not whate'er I knew before,
All that I hitherto had loved, believed,
And did I not thence follow in his steps,
Without complaint, like one who strays aside,
And by some traveller is shown the path?
And so, by strength of never-flagging will
And toil, achieved no mean success in art,
That knows no limit. Fame now smiled on me,
And in the hearts of men I found response
And answer to the fancies of my soul.
And I was happy, in my work took joy,
Found pleasure in my triumphs and my fame;
Took equal joy in work of other men,
My friends and fellows in the art divine.
And all that time not once I felt the pangs

Of grudgng envy; not when Piccini
Adroitly caught the ear of fickle France,
Or Iphigenia's first notes I heard.
Who says that Saglieri, in his pride,
Was then the slave of treacherous envy,
Like some foul snake that has been trodden on,
And, living still, in rage all impotent,
Will on his belly crawling, gnaw the dust?
Not one... but now... I myself proclaim it...
I grudge this man his fame... am filled with spite!
And where God's justice, if His greatest gift,
Undying genius, be curt refused
To warmest love, and sacrifice of self,
To labour, zeal, and supplicating cries,
And given to illume a trifler's head
With glory's halo?... Ah, Mozart! Mozart!
                              (Enters Mozart.)

MOZART.

And so, hast spied me out? Now, think, I wished
To give a good surprise, and play a trick.

SAGLIERI.

'Tis thou! Hast long been here?

MOZART.

                              I have just come
With something new that I would have thee hear;
But, passing on my road an alehouse, heard
A fiddler... but no! my Saglieri,
A droller thing, I ween, thou hast ne'er known!

Within the house I heard a fiddler blind
Play, *Voi che sapete.* Only think!
I could not help myself, have brought him here,
To give a taste of his high art. Here, you!
Come in!
(*A blind fiddler enters.*)
Now, play us something from Mozart!
(*Fiddler plays an air from Don Juan, whilst Mozart
listens and laughs.*)

SAGLIERI.

And thou canst laugh at that?

MOZART.

Why, even so!
And dost thou not thyself feel forced to laugh?

SAGLIERI.

And should I laugh when some sign-painter's man
Of Raphael's Madonna makes his daub?
Or should I laugh because some brainless clown
Has dared burlesque our Dante's mighty verse?
Away, old fool!

MOZART.

One moment, friend: take this,
And please to drink my health.
(*Fiddler goes out.*)
But as for thee,
I find thee out of humour now. I'll come
A fitter time.

SAGLIERI.

What hast thou brought with thee?

MOZART.

A trumpery nothing! The other night,
As I lay tossing in a sleepless fit,
There came into my head two, three phrases;
I wrote them down this morning, and would hear
Thy verdict on the piece. But not just now!
Thou art in no fit mind.

SAGLIERI.

Tell me, Mozart,
When thou wert not a welcome guest? Sit down!
I am all ears.
(*Mozart sits down at the piano.*)

MOZART.

And now, of some one think;
Whom shall I say?... Well, me... But not so old...
In love, not madly, but a slight attack,
With lady, or male friend... suppose, thyself...
And I'm all gay, when suddenly I see
In dream a coffin, cloud of thickest dark,
Or some weird thing. Now, listen, pray!
(*Begins to play*).

SAGLIERI.

And thou,
Mozart, wert hither on thy road with *that*,
And yet couldst loiter at a common inn,

And listen to a vagrant fiddler! God!
Mozart, thou art unworthy of thyself!

MOZART.

Well, what? Not bad? So, so?

SAGLIERI.

                      What depth of thought!
What boldness, and what harmony withal!
Thou art a God, Mozart, and dost not know!
But I and others know!

MOZART.

          Bah! As you like;
But, know, your hungry Godship fain would dine.

SAGLIERI.

Let us at the Golden Lion meet.

MOZART.

                        Agreed,
Agreed! But let me first go home and tell
The wife I shall not dine with her to-day.

SAGLIERI.

I will await thee; so, be sure to come.
                        (Exit Mozart.)
I can no longer strive against my fate:
It calls, and I, the chosen one, must check
His proud career; or else, we are undone,
All music's priests and ministers devout,

All, not I alone with my obscure fame.
What good can he achieve, though he should live,
And reach, perchance, yet higher, grander heights?
And does he think thereby to raise our art?
Vain dream! our art, when once he quits the scene,
Will fall again, since he can leave no heir.
What good can he bequeath? Like cherubim,
He brings with him from Paradise new strains,
But only that, when he has roused in us,
Poor, helpless children of our prison earth,
Hopes vague and wingless, he may fly away,
And leave us beggars as we were before!
This poison was Isora's dying gift:
Eighteen long years I have kept it hoarded,
Though life has often seemed a worthless boon.
When with my unsuspecting foe I sat,
And, gaily feasting, at one board caroused,
I ne'er have yielded to the tempter's voice.
And yet I feel scant love of life, and am
No coward prone to bear the sting of wrong.
But still I have deferred the fatal act,
And when the thirst of death most tortured me,
Have thought, why should I die? May be, that life
Will bring me yet the boon so long withheld;
May be, I too shall know those sleepless nights,
When brain is stirred with forms anew inspired;
May be, a second Haydn shall fresh create
A master-work wherein to find full joy.
When feasting with some hated rival-guest,
I thought, I have not found my dearest foe,
May be, some sharper wrong I must endure:
So, wait: and then Isora's gift will serve!

And I was right to wait! I have now found
My dearest foe, and now a second Haydn
Has made me drunk with heavenly rapture!
The hour has come: so, let the gift of love
In friendship's cup this day be boldly thrown!

SCENE THE SECOND.

A private room in an hotel with a piano.
Mozart and Saglieri sitting at a table.

SAGLIERI.

Wherefore so dull to-day?

MOZART.

I am not dull.

SAGLIERI.

Nay, nay, Mozart! There's something on thine heart.
A perfect dinner and superbest wine,
And there thou moping sitst!

MOZART.

I do confess,
My Requiem doth haunt and worry me.

SAGLIERI.

So, busy with a Requiem? Since when?

MOZART.

Some while, three weeks or more. But now a strange...
Have I not told thee?

SAGLIERI.

No.

MOZART.

It happened thus:
One night, three weeks ago, I late came home,
And learned a visitor had called on me.
I know not why, all night I sleepless lay,
And wondered who he was and what he would.
The stranger on the morrow came again;
Once more I chanced to be away from home.
The third day I was romping on the floor
With youngest boy, when our maid announced him.
I left the room, and found a stranger dressed
In sable suit, who prayed me write for him
A Requiem, and departed. That day
Began to write, but naught have seen since then,
Or heard of the strange visitor in black.
And I am glad, for it were hard to give
My work away, though finished now it be,
My Requiem. But none the less, I...

SAGLIERI.

What?

MOZART.

I am ashamed, my friend, to tell.

SAGLIERI.

> But what?

MOZART.

> This visitor unknown disturbs my rest;
> By day and night he haunts and follows me,
> As though he were my shadow. And e'en now,
> It seems that he, a third unbidden guest,
> Between us sits.

SAGLIERI.

> What childish fears! My friend,
> These gloomy fancies banish! Beaumarchais
> Was wont to say: Listen, Saglieri,
> When muddling thoughts oppress and trouble thee,
> At once uncork a bottle of champagne,
> Or read my *Mariage de Figaro*.

MOZART.

> Yes, Beaumarchais has ever been thy friend:
> 'Twas he who wrote the words for thy *Tarare*,
> A splendid piece of work. There is one air
> In gay and merry mood I often hum...
> But, Saglieri, is the story true,
> That, jealous, he a rival poisoned once?

SAGLIERI.

> The tale is false: the man is far too great
> A clown to practise such a trade!

MOZART.

                                Besides,
He is a génius, as thou and I;
Now, genius and ill can ne'er exist
In one and self-same soul. Is that not true?

SAGLIERI.

Thou thinkest so, Mozart?
                      (Pours poison into the wine.)
                           Well, drink, my friend!

MOZART.

Thy health and our sincerest union!
May Saglieri and Mozart, the friends
Of music, be in heart and soul close knit!
                                (He drinks).

SAGLIERI.

Stay!... Thou hast drunk... and drunk, not waiting me!

MOZART.

                   (Throwing down his napkin.)
Enough! No more!   *(Going to the piano.)*
                Listen, Saglieri!
                               (Begins to play.)
My Requiem!... What, dost thou weep?

SAGLIERI.

                              These tears
I shed, are both a pleasure and a pain;

As if I had some hardest task fulfilled,
As if the surgeon's knife had clean cut off
A gangrened limb. These tears, my dear Mozart,...
But pay no heed to them! Play on, play on,
And drown my soul in sweetest melody!

MOZART.

Would all thus felt the power of sweet sound!
But no! For, then, the world must need, perforce,
Come to an end: then, none would careful be
About the daily wants of sordid life,
And all would make themselves the priests of art.
But, as it is, we are the chosen few,
With scorn neglect the paltry gross of gain,
And live the prophets of the beautiful.
Is it not so?... But sick at heart I feel...
Something ails me... a trifle... I'll go home,
And sleep it off. Adieu!

SAGLIERI.

Farewell!
(Exit Mozart.)
Thy sleep,
Mozart, shall know no waking! Can it be,
That he is right, and I no genius?
„For genius and ill can ne'er exist
In one and self-same soul". But that is false!
And how Buonarroti? Or, is that
A stupid legend of the crowd... and he,
Who built the Vatican, no murderer?

THE BRONZE CAVALIER.

A POEM IN TWO CANTOS.

THE BRONZE CAVALIER.

PROLOGUE.

On the waste shore of raving waves
He stood, with high and dread thoughts filled,
And gazed afar. Before him rolled
The river wide, a fragile bark
Its tortuous path slow making.
Upon the moss-grown banks and swamps
Stood far asunder smoky huts,
The homes of Finnish fishers poor;
Whilst all around, a forest wild,
Unpierced by misty-circled sun,
Murmured loud.
   Gazing far, he thought:
From hence we can the Swede best threat;
Here must I found a city strong,
That shall our haughty foe bring ill;
It is by nature's law decreed,
That here we break a window through,
And boldly into Europe look,
And on the sea with sure foot stand;
By water path as yet unknown,
Shall ships from distant ports arrive,
And far and wide our reign extend.

A hundred years have passed, and now,
In place of forests dark and swamps,
A city new, in pomp unmatched,
Of Northern lands the pride and gem.
Where Finnish fisher once at eve,
Harsh nature's poor abandoned child,
From low-sunk boat was wont his net
With patient toil to cast, and drag
The stream, now stretch long lines of quays,
Of richest granite formed, and rows
Of buildings huge and lordly domes
The river front; whilst laden ships
From distant quarters of the world
Our hungry wharfs fresh spoils supply;
And needful bridge its span extends,
To join the stream's opposing shores;
And islets gay, in verdure clad,
Beneath the shade of gardens laugh.
Before the youthful city's charms
Her head proud Moscow jealous bends,
As when the new Tsaritza young
The widowed Empress lowly greets.

I love thee, work of Peter's hand!
I love thy stern, symmetric form;
The Neva's calm and queenly flow
Betwixt her quays of granite-stone,
With iron tracings richly wrought;
Thy nights so soft with pensive thought,
Their moonless glow, in bright obscure,
When I alone, in cosy room,
Or write or read, night's lamp unlit;

The sleeping piles that clear stand out
In lonely streets, and needle bright,
That crowns the Admiralty's spire:
When, chasing far the shades of night,
In cloudless sky of golden pure,
Dawn quick usurps the pale twilight,
And brings to end her half-hour reign.
I love thy winters bleak and harsh;
Thy stirless air fast bound by frosts;
The flight of sledge o'er Neva wide,
That glows the cheeks of maidens gay.
I love the noise and chat of balls;
A banquet free from wife's control,
Where goblets foam, and bright blue flame
Darts round the brimming punch-bowl's edge.
I love to watch the martial troops
The spacious Field of Mars fast scour;
The squadrons spruce of foot and horse;
The nicely chosen race of steeds,
As gaily housed they stand in line,
Whilst o'er them float the tattered flags;
The gleaming helmets of the men
That bear the marks of battle-shot.
I love thee, when with pomp of war
The cannons roar from fortress-tower;
When Empress-Queen of all the North
Hath given birth to royal heir;
Or when the people celebrate
Some conquest fresh on battle-field;
Or when her bonds of ice once more
The Neva, rushing free, upheaves,
The herald sure of spring's rebirth.

Fair city of the hero, hail!
Like Russia, stand unmoved and firm!
And let the elements subdued
Make lasting peace with thee and thine.
Let angry Finnish waves forget
Their bondage ancient and their feud;
Nor let them with their idle hate
Disturb great Peter's deathless sleep!

It was a day of fear and dread,
In book of memory still writ.
And now, for you, my friends, the tale
Of that day's woe I will begin;
And mournful will my story be.

CANTO THE FIRST.

    O'er Peter's cloud-wrapt city hung
November's autumn cold and mist.
With noisy splash of angry wave
The Neva chafed her granite fence,
As one, confined to bed with pain,
Will peevish toss from side to side.
The hour was late, and it was dark,
The rain beat hard on window-pane,
The wind with mournful howl roared loud,
When young Evjenie bade his friends
Adieu, and homeward turned his steps.
Evjenie is our hero's name,
A name that lightly falls in verse,
And one my pen is used to write.
No interest his surname has,
Though in the olden times gone by,
May be, it was in high repute;
We meet with it in Karamsin,
Like other once familiar names;
But now 'tis lost and all unknown.
In district called Kolumna lived
Our hero, who in office served.
His chiefs he feared, but patient bore

Death of relations dear and near,
Or world's neglect of service past.

 Evjenie reached his home, uphung
His cloak, undressed, and went to bed.
But long it was before he slept;
A host of cares possessed his brain.
He thought... of what? That he was poor
And hard must toil, if he would bare
Existence get, in freedom live,
Or have his neighbour's good repute.
Wished that God had but endowed him
With greater wit, or better, wealth;
For in our world are those who have
No wit, and never think to work,
And still contrive to live in ease;
Whilst he must drudge and slave, or starve.
And then, our hero heard the storm,
With fury lashed, still louder rage,
And thought the bridges soon across
The Neva wide would be removed,
And he for two or three whole days
Could of Parasha have no news.

 Such were his thoughts. And all that night
His heart within him ached. He prayed
The dreary wind would cease to howl,
The rain not beat on window-pane
So angrily.

   At length sleep closed
His heavy eyes. And now, the last

Dark scattered clouds of night began
To pale, as dawned the day of doom
And woe.

   All night the Neva wild
Had sought escape in open sea,
Till 'gainst the storm's mad rage to strive
She ceased, her strength completely broke.
At morn, along the river's shores,
The people thronged and watched with awe
The angry splash, the high-tossed foam,
And crested tops of heaving waves.
But stronger roared, with scream and wail,
The furious blast that river forced
Retreat, and break its confines low,
And drown the isles beneath its waves.
More fiercely still the storm-winds raged,
Insulted Neva shrieked with pain,
Its waters boiled and thundered high,
And, like wild beast escaped from cage,
Its ruin wide o'er city spread.
Before it fled the crowds, and all
Was one waste sea. The waters poured,
And forced their way through cellar-caves,
Beat down the rails of each canal,
Till Petropol, like Triton, stood
Plunged deep, breast-high, in ocean's storm.

  As in a leaguered town, the waves,
Like thieves, through windows burst, and sterns
Of boats in shivers broke the panes;
The awnings frail of fish-barks drenched,

The roofs and wreck of ruined homes,
The shopman's unsold stores and stock,
The year's hard savings of the poor,
The bridges from their moorings wrenched,
And coffins loose from churchyards torn,
Swam down the streets.

                      The maddened folk
In ruin's work God's wrath beheld,
And, trembling, ills yet greater waited;
For all was lost, nor could they hope
Fresh homes, or food, or help to find.

In that year of woe and horror,
Tsar Alexander ruled in fame.
From palace window, sick at heart
And grieved, he looked, and muttered low:
„Before dread Nature, might of Tsars
Is naught and vain!" And long he sate,
And, sobbing, watched the ruin spread.
The city squares were changed to lakes,
The streets in broad streams swam, and like
Abandoned isle the palace stood.
Then spake the Tsar.... From point to point,
Along the near and distant streets
Two tried and trusty lords, in boat
Began to make their dang'rous way
To save the wretches lost in fear,
And drowning in their battered homes.

Meanwhile in Petroff's gloomy square,
Where the new, huge building rises,

And where, on either side of porch,
There stands, on pedestal high reared,
With upraised paw, as large as life,
A lion guardian, on the watch:
Upon the brute's wide marble back,
Without a cap, hands clasped round mane,
Evjenie sate, all pale and still.
And if his cheeks were wan with fright,
It was not for himself he feared.
He had not seen the thirsty waves
Loud howling rise above his feet;
Nor felt the torrents lash his face;
Nor heard the sharp, grim shriek of wind,
That caught and tossed his cap away.
His eyes despairingly were fixed
On one far spot, where mountain-high
From deep abyss the waters climbed,
And, dashing down, before them bore
The floating wrecks of waste and spoil.
Great God! 'twas where they strove most fierce,
The central point of their blind force,
On brink of widely swollen gulf,
An old house stood, with willow-tree
Before and wooden fence, the home
Of widow poor and daughter fair,
His life's one hope.... Or did he rave,
And was it all mere fancy's trick?
Or is our life an empty dream,
The toy and sport of jesting fate?...
And there, as bound by some strong spell,
Or chained to marbled lion's back,
He sate, and could not stir. Around

Was water, water, nothing else.
And all the while, face turned from him,
Supreme on safe, defiant height,
Above the stir of troubled waves,
Sate, with his royal hand outstretched,
The giant on his steed of bronze.

CANTO THE SECOND.

At length, with work of ruin tired,
Her mutiny the Neva ceased,
And to her former course returned,
In mere revolt her pleasure found,
And careless left her prey behind.
As on an unprotected town
Armed brigands fall, and rob and kill,
And naught is heard but cries of grief
And rage, vain threats, and panic shrieks,
Whilst havoc uncontrolled prevails,
Till glut of spoil and fear of law
Disarm the thieves, who home retreat
And half their booty leave in fright.

The waters fell, the vanished roads
Once more appeared. With sinking heart,
Evjenie, half in hope, in fear
And anguish, neared the scarce calmed gulf.
Proud of their strength, its sullen waves
Muttered and surged, as if beneath
Some angry fire still smouldered deep;
And fast they rolled in foaming rage,

And heavily the Neva breathed,
Like panting steed that flies the field.
Evjenie looks, and boat discerns,
And runs as to a treasure found;
In haste he calls the boatman near,
Who, bargaining, consents to bring
Our hero o'er the storm-tossed stream.

    And long with tempest-driven waves
The skilful oarsman battling strove,
And oft the boat is sinking lost,
And hurled beneath the cloud-capped crests,
As oft upbounds... until at length
It touched the shore.

                        The well-known street
And friendly spot are eager sought.
But dazed he looks, for all is changed,
And awful is the sight revealed.
A mass of ruins lies before,
In part thrown down, in part waste blank,
Houses falling, or laid quite prone,
Whilst some are scattered by the waves,
— Like corpses left on battle-field
To rot. Headlong, Evjenie sped,
Scarce knowing why or where he rushed,
And ill forebodings weighed his heart.
——And now he comes where fate awaits,
As with sealed letter in her hand.
The intervening space is passed,
With hastened step he nears the house:
But what is this he sees?

He stopped...
Retreated... and once more returned...
Bewildered gazed... went on... looked back.
Here is the place their house once stood,
And there the willow-tree. The gates
Here entrance barred. But where the house?
Thoughts of horror now possessed him,
As round and round he marched and stared.
While whirling words broke from his lips,
And with clenched fist his forehead struck,
And sudden shrieked with laughter loud.

Once more, the friendly shades of night
The city fearsome shroud, but few
Their couches sought, and long discussed
Among themselves, with bated breath,
That day of woe.

Clear morning's ray
From out the pale and wearied clouds
The fated city gleamed to cheer.
But few the traces were it found
Of past night's wreck. With purple pall
The ugly work of ill was hid,
And life resumed its wonted ways.
Again the free and open streets
Were thronged with crowds intent on self,
And none to give the dead a thought.
The sleek-dressed clerk for office left
His home. The tradesman, unabashed,
His courage kept and oped his vaults
The Neva had despoiled, and schemed

How best he could his neighbour make
Redeem his loss. The cumbered yards
Of boats were cleared.

                        And Count Chvostoff,
Poet inspired by heavenly muse,
In verse immortal, though unread,
Failed not to sing of Neptune's wrath.

But poor Evjenie, what of him?
His mind was tender, easy touched,
Nor proof against these griefful woes.
The horrid noise of rebel waves
And winds loud echoed in his ears.
Aimless, he wandered here and there,
Strange thoughts revolving in his mind,
He ne'er could solve. A demon dream
Haunted, followed, and possessed him.
A week, a month went by, and he
Still heedless roamed, nor home returned;
The term elapsed, his room was let
To tenant new, poor as himself,
Nor did he come his goods to fetch,
But soon was lost to world and men.
All day the streets he idly strayed,
And slept at night in wharf or shed,
His food, the crust of bread he begged.
His well-worn cloak in tatters hung
Each day more loose. And wanton boys
Their play would cease, to hurl sharp stones,
As he passed by, and coachmen rude
With whip aroused him from his daze,

As in mid-road he puzzled stood;
And on he moved without complaint:
A voice within, unheard of men,
Had deafened him to outer noise.
And so he lived, like one that is
Nor beast nor man, nor live nor dead,
Nor denizen of earth, nor ghost
Of other world.

          By river-side,
He once was sleeping in a wharf;
The trees had cast their summer dress,
And autumn winds begun to blow.
The angry surge beat on the wharf,
Nor ceased to dash against its steps;
As widow knocked importunate
At the unrighteous judge's door.
He woke. But all was dark and dull;
The rain fell fast; the shrill blasts wailed;
And in the distance he could hear
The echo low of sentry's voice.
Up leaped Evjenie; he recalled
The horrors of the past, and rose,
His aimless roamings to resume.
But suddenly he paused, and with
Large eyes of fear he slowly scanned
The dreary space that stretched around.
He found himself beneath the porch
Of spacious house. And on the steps,
With upraised paws, as large as life,
Two lions stood, both keeping guard:
Whilst in the darkness, tow'ring high,

On pedestal of granite rock,
Sate, with his royal hand outstretched,
The giant on his steed of bronze.

Evjenie shuddered, and his thoughts
Grew strangely clear. Again he saw
The place where seas had wildly played,
Where waves of prey had shrieking roared,
And round him dashed with angry whirl:
He saw the lions, square, and *him*,
Who with bronze head, and motionless,
In the darkness proudly towered,
As ever, with his hand outstretched,
He watched the city he had built.

The poor mad creature wildly roamed
Around the rock with aching limbs.
And read the words clear cut in stone;
And, crushed with grief, his bleeding heart
Grew dead within him. And he pressed
His burning brow against the rail;
A blinding mist came o'er his eyes,
And through his frame a shudder ran,
As he stood trembling, lost in gloom,
Before great Russia's giant Tsar.
With finger raised in dumb reproach,
He thought' to speak. But no word came.
And quick he took to headlong flight.
It seemed, his face with angry glow
Aflame, the all-dread Tsar had turned,
And fixed on him his searching gaze:
He fled, and, flying, heard behind,

Like roll of thunder, loud and sharp,
The heavy measured tread of feet,
That shook the ground beneath their march:
And in the pale moon's silver light,
With hand majestic, far outstretched,
The Statue Knight of Bronze pursued,
High mounted on his lordly steed.
And all that night the crazed wretch heard,
Where'er he sped his flying steps,
In close pursuit the Knight of Bronze,
And measured tramp of prancing steed.
And from that day, if e'er he chanced
To cross the square where statue stood,
A troubled stare came o'er his face,
And quick he pressed to heart his hand,
As if to quell some sharpest pain,
And well-worn cap from head removed,
Nor daring raise his fear-struck eyes,
In stealth slunk by.

     Close to the beach,
An island small is seen. And there
Belated fisher anchor casts,
And frugal evening meal prepares;
Or spruce-dressed citizen in boat,
Decked out for Sunday trip, will touch
The lone abandoned isle, where not
A blade of grass redeems the waste.
'Twas there the waters, when they fell,
The widow's house had stranded left;
And like black bush it rose above
Their surface, till in early spring

Men came and carted it away.
It was all bare, nor found they aught,
Save our friend, poor mad Evjenie,
On the threshold fallen. And there.
With friendly hands, his corpse they laid.

THE STATUE GUEST.

A DRAMATIC SKETCH IN FOUR SCENES.

THE STATUE GUEST.

SCENE THE FIRST.

Night. A Cemetry near Madrid.

DON JUAN.

Here will we wait the night. At last, thank God,
Before us lies Madrid. And soon, once more,
Its streets and squares familiar I shall roam,
In cloak my face concealed and cap down drawn;
What sayst? Methinks, I shall be here unknown.

LEPORELLO.

To know Don Juan here discernment needs!
The place is crammed with fellows like himself.

DON JUAN.

Thou speakst in jest. Who is there will know me?

LEPORELLO.

The first old watchman that we chance to meet,
Or drunken player of the serenade,
Or cavalier, spruce rival of your trade,
Well cloaked and masked, with sword beneath his arm.

DON JUAN.

 And what great harm, if they discover me?
We must avoid the King, and for the rest,
There is not one I fear in all Madrid.

LEPORELLO.

 Before to-morrow the King will know
That of your own free will you have returned,
And in Madrid your pranks will play. But say,
What will the King now do?

DON JUAN.

       Why, send me back!
'Tis sure he will not care to take my head;
Of all state-crimes I'm innocent, and if
He banished me, it was from love, to save
Me from the slain man's kin and friends.

LEPORELLO.

         Just so!
And there you might have lived in quiet ease.

DON JUAN.

 I humbly thank thee! Why, man, I well nigh
Died of spleen and dulness there! Oh, those men,
That country, sky like canopy of smoke,
And then the women! Well I ne'er would change,
My friend, the lowest-born or clumsiest
Of all the maids of Andalusia
For first and proudest of their stately dames!
Awhile, 'tis true, their large blue eyes, soft traits,

And bearing coy and modest, did possess
The charm of something novel and untried;
But soon, thank God, I felt it were a sin
To lose one's heart to women such as they:
No breathers, but mere statues, dolls of wax,
Whilst ours... But hark, this place, it seems, to us
Is known, or dost thou fail remember it?

LEPORELLO.

Can I forget? The convent is well known,
And well remembered. When you hither came
In yonder grove the horses I must hold;
No cheerful task, you will confess. Your time
Was spent more gay than mine!

DON JUAN.

My poor Inez!
She is no more! But ne'er was love more true.
'Twas in July, one night. A wondrous joy
I found in her sad, shrouded glance, and lips
Of death-pale hue. Methought it strange, but thou,
It seems, her beauty rare wouldst ne'er confess.
In truth, 'twere hard to find in her one trait,
That faultless could be called. But, man, her eyes,
Her eyes, and with that glance!... A glance like hers,
I think, I never since have seen! Her voice
Was low and weak, a sickly woman's voice...
Her husband was a scoundrel and a brute,
I later learned... Alas, my poor Inez!

LEPORELLO.

Maids fairer than Inez have ta'en her place.

DON JUAN.
'Tis true!

LEPORELLO.
And, if we live, new queens shall reign!

DON JUAN.
And that is also true.

LEPORELLO.
And now, who is
The favoured one we have to seek?

DON JUAN.
                    Laura!
To her my homage straight I pay.

LEPORELLO.
                    Agreed!

DON JUAN.
At once I fly to her; and if I find
Some busy fool my visit has forestalled,
I'll pray her leap through window to my arms!

LEPORELLO.
Of course! And so, fresh pleasures we will seek,
Nor shall the dead long haunt to trouble us!
But who comes here?   *(Enters Monk).*

MONK.
                She will be here at once.
But who are these? The Lady Anna's men?

LEPORELLO.

No serfs are we, but strangers hither come
To see Madrid.

DON JUAN.

And whom may you await?

MONK.

It is the hour the Lady Anna fixed
Her husband's tomb to visit.

DON JUAN.

                How, Lady
De Solva, the wife of the Commander,
Who killed in duel was, by whom I have
Forgot?

MONK.

By Don Juan, the godless wretch.

LEPORELLO.

'Tis strange, but true; through thickest convent
                                    walls
Our gallant Juan's fame has made its way,
And hermits grave do sing the hero's praise.

MONK.

May be, he's known to you?

LEPORELLO.

                      We know him not;
But, pray, where is he now?

MONK.

     No longer here,
But far in exile lives.

LEPORELLO.

     And God be praised!
The farther off the better. Would such rogues
Were in one common sack cast in the sea!

     DON JUAN. *(Aside to Leporello.)*
What folly pratest thou?

     LEPORELLO. *(Aside to Don Juan.)*
     Hush! on purpose....

DON JUAN.

And so, 'tis here the poor Commander lies!

MONK.

Here. The wife a monument has founded,
And hither, robed in black, each day she comes,
To pray his sinful, erring soul repose,
And o'er his grave to weep.

DON JUAN.

     A widow strange!
The lady's spouse with jealousy was mad,
And kept her under lock and close confined;
Not one of us e'er caught a glance of her.
But men report her fair.

MONK.

              Our oath forbids
That we in woman's beauty take delight;
But sin it is to lie, nor sourest saint
Would care deny the lady's wondrous charms.

DON JUAN.

It is my wish to speak with her a word.

MONK.

Vain wish: with men she never holds commune.

DON JUAN.

Not e'en with you, most reverend father?

MONK.

With me she may and does, for I am monk.
But look, she comes.   *(Enters Donna Anna.)*

DONNA ANNA.

The gate, my father, ope.

MONK.

At once, signora, here I've waited thee.
        (Donna Anna follows the monk.)

LEPORELLO.

And pray, what kind of beauty is she?

DON JUAN.

                        Naught
Could see beneath the close-drawn widow veil;
Though well I marked a graceful little foot.

LEPORELLO.

That is enough! At once your fancy fires,
And in a minute nimbly draws the rest;
Ne'er painter had a phantasy so keen.
No matter, how or where you may begin,
With lady's brow or with her foot.

DON JUAN.
> Hearken.
I will with her acquaintance make.

LEPORELLO. *(Aside)*.
> I fain
Would know the why! The husband he has killed,
And now, forsooth, the widow's tears must see:
Oh, shameless wretch!

DON JUAN.
> It is already dusk,
And till the moon attains her full mid course,
Making the shades of night a clear obscure,
We'll freely stroll Madrid's wide streets.

LEPORELLO. *(Aside)*.
> Like thief,
The Spanish gallant hotly waits the night,
And fears the moon. By heaven, a cursed life!
Must I much longer yet be tied to him?
My strength begins to fail to keep his pace

SCENE THE SECOND.

A Room. Supper-party at Laura's.

FIRST GUEST.

I swear, I never yet have known thee play
With taste so finished and so natural,
Each little detail of the part well seized.

SECOND GUEST.

How well developed! with what force and fire!

THIRD GUEST.

And with what grace and art

LAURA.

       Myself I felt.
In each word and movement I was inspired;
The words flowed forth direct, unsought, their source
The heart, and not the halting memory.

FIRST GUEST.

'Tis true, and even now thine eyes gleam bright,
Thy cheeks are flushed, thy frame with passion moved,
Let not the fire burn dull, but, Laura, sing,
Sing another song.

LAURA.

Give me the guitar.
(Plays and sings).

ALL.

Oh, bravo! bravo! marvellous! splendid!

FIRST GUEST.

We thank thee, fair enchantress! Thou hast charmed
Our hearts. Methinks, of all the joys of life,
To love alone must music yield its place;
And yet, not so, for love is music!... Look,
Don Carlos, the morose, himself is touched.

SECOND GUEST.

How rich in tone! How grandly full of soul!
But, Laura, whose the words?

LAURA.

Don Juan's words.

DON CARLOS.

How, Don Juan?

LAURA.

Yes, 'tis he who wrote them,
Truest friend, and lover most inconstant!

DON CARLOS.

A Godless brigand is thy Don Juan,
And thyself a little fool!

LAURA.

Art thou mad?
Another word, my servants will I call
To oust thee hence, however high thy rank!

DON CARLOS.

Call, if thou wilt!

FIRST GUEST.

I pray thee, Laura, cease!
Don Carlos, calm thy rage! She did forget....

LAURA.

Forget? That he in fair and open fight
His brother killed? 'Tis him he should have slain!

DON CARLOS.

I own, 'twas folly thus to rage and fume.

LAURA.

'Tis well: if thou thyself thy folly ownst,
Then peace is made.

DON CARLOS.

I am alone to blame:
Forgive me, but thou knowst I ne'er can hear
Unmoved the brigand Juan's hated name.

LAURA.

Am I in fault, if Juan's name, unsought,
From time to time thus rises to my lips?

FIRST GUEST.

To prove thine anger has already passed,
Another song we pray.

LAURA.

The last to-night,
'Tis late, full time to part. What shall I sing?
Ah, listen!

ALL.

Delightful! charming! perfect!

LAURA.

And now, farewell, good friends!

GUESTS.

Farewell, our thanks!
(*Exeunt guests. Laura detains Don Carlos.*)

LAURA.

Nay, thou, mad friend, must here remain to-night;
There's much in thee I like: thou dost remind me
Of Don Juan when thou dost rail at me,
Or grindst thy teeth with rage.

DON CARLOS.

Happy Juan!
And didst thou love this Juan?
(*Laura nods her head.*)
What, much?

LAURA.

Much!

DON CARLOS.

And lovst him now?

LAURA.

Now? this very minute?
Nay, nay, I cannot love two men at once.
Thou art my lover now.

DON CARLOS.

Tell me, Laura,
Thou hast how many years?

LAURA.

I am eighteen.

DON CARLOS.

Thou art a child in years... and wilt be young
Some five or six years more. And all around thee
For these six years will crowd and worship thee,
Will flatter, fondle, make thee rich with gifts,
With rhyming serenades will soothe thy sleep,
And savage duels fight where crossways meet;
But, Laura, when these years have passed, thine eyes
Lack lustre, and their lids are dull and morne,
When silver gray doth mingle with thy brown,
And men begin to speak of thee as old;
Then... what wilt thou say?

LAURA.

Then... but wherefore think
Of what may be? A subject strange to choose!
Or dost thou like to muse what fate may bring?

But come, the balcony we'll open wide.
How calm the sky! Naught stirs the balmy air!
The night is sweetly heavy with the scent
Of laurel and the citron; the cloudless moon
Shines bright, and lightens up the deep dark blue;
The drowsy watchman sounds his warning cry;
And all is peace around us! But elsewhere,
In the far distant north,... at Paris, say,...
A cold rain, drizzling, beats, and bleak winds blow:
It hurts us not. And, therefore, listen, friend,
Look bright, and careless smile. 'Tis my command:
That is well!

DON CARLOS.

Enchantress queen!
(*A knock is heard.*)

DON JUAN.

Laura, hey!

LAURA.

Who knocks? Whose voice is that?

DON JUAN.

Hey, open quick!

LAURA.

Great heavens, 'tis he!
(*Opens door: enters Don Juan.*)

DON JUAN.

Good morrow!

LAURA.

(*Throwing herself on his neck.*)
Don Juan!

DON CARLOS.

How so? Don Juan!

DON JUAN.   (*Kissing Laura.*)
Laura, darling mine!
But who is with thee?

DON CARLOS.

'Tis I, Don Carlos!

DON JUAN.

An undesired and unwelcome meeting!
I'm at your service, Don, to-morrow morn.

DON CARLOS.

Nay, now, this minute!

LAURA.

Cease, Don Carlos, cease!
Here is no place to brawl! Thou art my guest!
I pray thee go at once!

DON CARLOS.

(*Not heeding Laura.*)
I wait, signor.
I see, thou hast a sword.

DON JUAN.

. Thou dost insist?
I will not thwart thee.

LAURA.

Have pity, Juan!
(*Laura falls back on her couch. Carlos is wounded.*)

DON JUAN.

Rise, Laura, rise! Tis done!

LAURA.

What do I see?
Don Carlos slain, and in my room! 'Tis well,
Thou cut-throat devil! What can I do now?
Or whither shall we lug this corpse?

DON JUAN.

May be,
He is not dead.   (*Examines the body.*)

LAURA.

Thou speakest truth, he breathes!
See, wretch! Straight through the heart thou hast
                              struck home,
And from the ugly wound no blood has flown;
And he no longer breathes! What hast thou done?

DON JUAN.

What could I do? He brought it on himself.

LAURA.

They grieve me much, these tricks of fortune blind,
And all no fault of thine!... But whence art thou?
How long hast thou returned?

DON JUAN.

But just arrived,
In hiding too; I am yet under ban.

LAURA.

Of Laura, then, were thy first thoughts, Juan?
Take my warmest thanks! And yet, beshrew me,
No single word thou sayst do I believe.
As thou wert passing down the street by chance,
My house recalled me to thy thoughts.

DON JUAN.

Nay, nay!
Demand of Leporello. He can tell
How I beyond the town in vilest inn
Have lodged, that I my Laura's home might seek.
(*He kisses her.*)

LAURA.

My truest, best of friends! But stay... the dead
Is with us here... what shall we do with him?

DON JUAN.

There let him lie... Before the dawn doth peep
I will convey him forth beneath my cloak,
And on a cross-road leave him.

LAURA.

                          Take good heed,
That none is near to see thee at thy work;
'Tis well thou didst not hither sooner come,
Some friends of mine have supped with me. They
                                            went
But just before thy knock. But only think,
If thou by evil chance hadst met them here!

DON JUAN.

    Laura, it is long that thou hast loved him?

LAURA.

    Loved whom? Art mad?

DON JUAN.

                       And tell me too, how oft
Thou hast contrived to cheat and play me false,
In my long absence forced?

LAURA.

                And thou, madcap?

DON JUAN.

    Nay, tell, I say... But no!.., Of that anon.

SCENE THE THIRD.

At the Monument in memory of the Commander.

DON JUAN.

Well, all has happened for the best! I killed
Unwittingly Don Carlos, and now, disguised
In hermit's serge, am blest each day with sight
Of Anna, fairest widow, and, methinks,
Her interest have won. Till now, we have
Exchanged salutes decorous; but to-day,
I'll break the ice and converse hold with her.
But how begin? „May I presume?" Or else,
„Signora fair!" Or what the brain suggests?
I'll speak whate'er I think and sing of love
The unpremeditated song that burns.
The hour has struck when she should come. I ween,
Her absence makes the poor Commander dull.
How grand the imperial air he assumes,
In breadth of shoulders, firm, a Hercules!
He was in form and soul a puny man,
Though here, on tiptoe standing, none can reach,
With hand uplifted, the Commander's nose.
When once behind the Escural we met,
With my sharp sword he was transpierced and fixed,

Like dragon-fly with needle pinned; and yet,
Proud he was and rash, in spirit cruel...
But here she comes.   (*Enters Donna Anna.*)

DONNA ANNA.

Again I meet him here!
I pray you, father, pardon me, if I
Disturb you from your pious thoughts.

DON JUAN.

Nay, I
Of you should pardon beg, lest, unwilling,
My presence here prevents free flow of grief.

DONNA ANNA.

Alas, my sorrow is within me locked.
With your kind aid my prayers to heaven may mount,
Alone, they are fast tied to earth. I pray,
Your griefful prayers to mingle with my woe.

DON JUAN.

I? I pray with you, good Donna Anna!
I am no worthy partner in thy prayers.
Nor with unholy lips will I presume
Repeat your words of earnest, sacred prayer:
But, rather, from afar with worship gaze,
And humbly watch, as, low in silence bent,
The marble pale with raven locks you sweep;
Whilst it shall seem to me, an angel blest
Hath on this tomb alighted, bringing peace.
Nor dare I hope in troubled heart to find
Fit words for prayer, but will silent wonder

How blest is he whose marble cold is warmed
With breath divine and dewed with tears of love.

DONNA ANNA.

Strange and puzzling words are these!

DON JUAN.

       Signora!

DONNA ANNA

It seems... You have forgotten...

DON JUAN.

      What? That I
A hermit pious am? that sinful voice
In such a place must not so freely speak?

DONNA ANNA.

It seemed to me... I did not understand...

DON JUAN.

Ah, I see, you have all, all discovered!

DONNA ANNA.

Discovered what?

DON JUAN.

    That I no monk can be,
And lowly at your feet I pardon seek.

DONNA ANNA.

Great heavens! arise, arise! Who are you, then?

DON JUAN.

A wretch, the victim of a hopeless love!

DONNA ANNA.

Oh God! that here, before this very grave...
Begone!

DON JUAN.

One short minute, lady, grant me!
A single word.

DONNA ANNA.

But should we be surprised?

DON JUAN.

The gate is locked. Grant but one short minute!

DONNA ANNA.

But say, what would you? What is your prayer?

DON JUAN.

                                             Death!
'Tis at your feet here kneeling I would die!
But let my poor, vile dust be laid to rest,
Not near the dust of him who boasts your love;
Not there, not near, but in some distant spot,
There, by the gate, upon its very threshold,
So that the stone above my grave may feel
The touch of foot, the rustle light of robe,
When hither you shall come, on that proud tomb
To lay those raven locks and silent weep.

DONNA ANNA.

'Tis madness prompts you thus to speak!

DON JUAN.

To die is madness sign, Donna Anna?
Were I but mad, I should desire to live;
Were I but mad, I should be buoyed with hope,
And trust to touch your heart with vows of love
Were I but mad, I should before your house
Long vigils keep and haunt your sleep with song;
Were I but mad, I should not hide, but seek
To live each minute near, within your glance;
Were I but mad, I should not e'er consent
To pine in silence!

DONNA ANNA.

Is this what you call
Silence!

DON JUAN.

A happy chance, a happy chance
Has tempted me to speak! Else never had
You known the sacred secret of my heart.

DONNA ANNA.

Tell me, is it long you have thus loved me?

DON JUAN.

Myself I know not be it long or not;
But from that hour I only know the price
Of our short life, and only from that hour
I know the wondrous bliss that life can give.

DONNA ANNA.

Go, leave me! You are a dangerous man!

DON JUAN.

And what fear you?

DONNA ANNA.

I fear your whirring words.

DON JUAN.

I will not speak; but banish not the man
Who in your presence finds his only joy:
No bold hopes presumptious do I nourish,
No favours ask I, but I must see you,
If only I be doomed to live.

DONNA ANNA.

Leave me!
No fitting place is this for such mad speech...
To-morrow come; and if you first will swear
To guard the reverence you show me here,...
The evening... later... I will receive you;
Though since the day a widow I became,
To all my doors are closed.

DON JUAN.

Angel Anna!
May God bless you, as you to-day have deigned
To give full comfort to my suff'ring heart.

DONNA ANNA.

And now you must depart.

DON JUAN.

> One minute more!

DONNA ANNA.

Full time it is for me to go; the more,
I cannot pray to-day: with worldly speech,
To which my ears have long, long been unused,
You have enticed me from religion's task.
To-morrow I'll receive you.

DON JUAN.

> Can it be?

Mine ears refuse belief. Nor dare I trust
The promised boon. To-morrow eve with you,
Not here, and not in stealth!

DONNA ANNA.

> I await you.

But your name?

DON JUAN.

> Diego di Calviedo.

DONNA ANNA.

Farewell, dear Don!

> (*Exit Donna Anna.*)

DON JUAN.

> Eh, Leporello, here!

LEPORELLO.

Your orders, signor?

DON JUAN.

     Ah, Leporello,
The gods are kind! „To-morrow evening, late:"
Thou hearst? To-morrow eve! All ready make!
Like some spoiled child, I'm wild with joy.

    LEPORELLO.

        Which means,
You greeted have the Donna Anna fair:
May be, two friendly words she spoke to you,
Or, perchance, you priestly blessing gave her.

    DON JUAN.

 Nay, Leporello, nay! 'Tis she who fixed
The hour of our meeting.

    LEPORELLO.

     It cannot be.
Oh widows, one and all both false and frail!

    DON JUAN.

 I'm mad with joy! I could the world embrace!

    LEPORELLO.

 But the Commander, what says he to this?

    DON JUAN.

 And dost thou fear that he will jealous prove?
But he is wiser now, a man of sense,
And death has taught him take things easily.

    LEPORELLO.

 But look upon his statue there!

DON JUAN.

                And what?

LEPORELLO.

It seems to me, with angry glance he looks
At you.

DON JUAN.

    Well, go, good Leporello, quick:
To be my guest invite him... no, not mine;...
Bid him come to Anna's house to-morrow.

LEPORELLO.

A statue ask? But with what aim?

DON JUAN.

                Well, not
That he may have the chance to speak with her!
To-morrow evening bid him thither come,
And at the door stand sentinel.

LEPORELLO.

            You jest,
But think, with whom.

DON JUAN.

    I bid thee go.

LEPORELLO.

              But...

DON JUAN.

                Go!

LEPORELLO.

           (*Going up to the monument.*)
Accept my greeting, statue fair and dread!
My lord, Don Juan, humbly begs you come
To Don... but no! the rest I dare not speak.
With fear I quake.

DON JUAN.

    Go on!

LEPORELLO.

           Thy will be done.
My lord, Don Juan, invites you visit
Your widow's house to-morrow evening late
There sentinel to stand.
           (*The statue bows in consent.*)
    Ah!

DON JUAN.

           What has happed?

LEPORELLO.

Horror! Spare me, great God!

DON JUAN.

           What ails thee, fool?

LEPORELLO.

           (*Pointing towards the statue.*)
The statue, look!

DON JUAN.

    But say, didst thou salute?

LEPORELLO.

Not I, but it.

DON JUAN.

What folly dost thou prate?

LEPORELLO.

Go yourself!

DON JUAN.

(*Going up to the statue.*)
Agreed, and look, vile coward!
I, great Commander, humbly pray thee be
At thy wife's house to-morrow eve, and there
At door keep watch as sentinel. Reply,
Wilt thou?...   (*Statue bows in assent.*)
Oh God!

LEPORELLO.

Well, what?

DON JUAN.

Let us begone!

SCENE THE FOURTH.

A Room in Donna Anna's House.

DONNA ANNA.

Welcome, Don Diego, though much I fear,
My sad and ever melancholy talk
Will weary you. For in my widowed state
My loss I ne'er forget: but tears with smiles
Like an April day do strangely mingle:
But silent why?

DON JUAN.

With words I dare not break
The silence of my joy: to be alone with you,
With you, dear friend, be with you here... not there,
Too close the dead man's grave, who won your love;
No longer do I see you on your knees
Before your marble spouse.

DONNA ANNA.

It cannot be,
That, like a girl, Diego jealous is,
Or that a buried husband tortures him.

DON JUAN.

I have no cause, I know, for jealousy:
But yet your spouse you chose him.

DONNA ANNA.

Nay, my hand
To Don Alvar my mother bade me give:
Remember, we were poor, and Alvar rich.

DON JUAN.

Happy man! his treasured dross he offered
Before the shrine of fairest goddess,
And won the joys of paradise. Had I
But seen you first, with what unmeasured pride
My rank, my wealth, my all I rendered had,
And been the slave officious of your will,
To snatch from you a single glance of love!
I would have quickly learned how best forestall
The slightest, smallest fancy of your soul,
And bask your life in cloudless sunshine bright!
Alas, that fate should thwart our best desires!

DONNA ANNA.

Diego, cease; It is a grievous sin
Such words to hearken.... I may not love you;
A widow must be faithful to the grave.
Could you but know how truly Don Alvar
Did love me! Don Alvar, my heart knows well,
Had never to his oath unloyal proved:
But hand in hand with love his marriage vow
Had gone.

DON JUAN.

      Do not, I pray, torment me more
With fond remembrances of days gone by.
Dear Donna Anna, cease to punish me,
Though punishment I have deserved

DONNA ANNA.

                           In what?
You are not bound by any sacred tie,
And none has claim on you. In loving me,
You have not sinned 'gainst me or heaven's law.

DON JUAN.

  Not sinned 'gainst you? Oh God!

DONNA ANNA.

                      What wrong have you
Done me? In what to blame? I bid thee, tell.

DON JUAN.

  Nay, ask me not!

DONNA ANNA.

              Diego, what means this?
In what are you to blame, I once more ask.

DON JUAN.

  I cannot, dare not.

DONNA ANNA.

             This is very strange:
I pray, demand, that you should tell.

DON JUAN.
Not I.

DONNA ANNA.

Is this your proffered, blind obedience?
And all that you but now did hotly swear?
You swore to be my slave. Then, answer me.
In what are you to blame?

DON JUAN.
I dare not say.
I would not have your hate.

DONNA ANNA.
Heark, Diego,
I swear, my fullest pardon shall not fail:
But I must know.

DON JUAN.
Be wise, and never learn
The hateful, deadly secret of my heart.

DONNA ANNA.

Your words are wild, they trouble me, and fill
My soul with horror vague. Nor can I guess
In what you have offended me. I knew
You not till yestermorn, and have no foes
Save one alone, the murd'rer of my spouse.

DON JUAN. *(Aside.)*

The hour has come.
One thing I fain would ask:
(Aloud.)

Don Juan, of men the most unhappy,
Is known to you?

DONNA ANNA.

I neither know, nor have
I ever seen him.

DON JUAN.

And in your heart of hearts,
You hate and loathe the man?

DONNA ANNA.

In honour bound.
But you would deftly turn me from my end!
Once more...

DON JUAN.

And if, by chance, you met Don Juan?

DONNA ANNA.

My dagger I would plunge into his heart!

DON JUAN.

Where is your dagger then? Here is my breast!

DONNA ANNA.

What mean these words? Speak, I pray, Diego!

DON JUAN.

No Diego, I!... I am Don Juan!

DONNA ANNA.

Oh God! you play with me! It cannot be!

DON JUAN.

I am Don Juan!

DONNA ANNA.

It is false!

DON JUAN.

     I killed
Your husband, nor pretend regret my deed;
No rebel sting of conscience do I feel.

DONNA ANNA.

What do I hear? Nay, nay, it cannot be!

DON JUAN.

Lady, Don Juan it is who loves thee.

DONNA ANNA.

Where am I? What do I hear? I faint!

DON JUAN.

        Heavens!
What have I done? What ails thee, Donna Anna?
Recall thy wand'ring thoughts! Thy Diego,
Thy loving slave is at thy feet!

DONNA ANNA.

    Leave me!

My foe, indeed, thou art. 'Tis thou who stole
All, all I had in life.

DON JUAN.

    Fairest being!
That fatal blow I long to expiate;
And at thy feet thy bidding humbly wait.
Say but the word,... I die; bid live,... I live,
Live but for thee.

DONNA ANNA.

  And so, thou art Don Juan.

DON JUAN.

 I know, thou hast been taught to hold me as
A cruel, monstrous wretch, and, lady fair,
I have, may be, deserved my evil fame;
May be, my conscience, stained and burdened sore,
Is weighted with much ill; but from the hour
I first saw thee, all is changed within me!
It seems to me I am in soul new born.
In loving thee, I also love the good,
And now do I first bend my trembling knee
In homage low before fair virtue's shrine.

DONNA ANNA.

 Don Juan, thou art eloquent, I know;
I've heard of thy glib tongue and cunning wile:
Men say, thou art a godless libertine,
And fierce. Canst count the list of women poor
Thou hast destroyed?

DON JUAN.
              Not one, believe, till now,
Not one of them I loved.

DONNA ANNA.
              Shall I believe
That Juan never loved, nor hopes to find
In me the newest victim of his lust?

DON JUAN.
And had I sought deceive thee, lady fair,
Should I have thus my name revealed, a name
Which thou, I know full well, art loath to hear?
In what, I pray, consists my treachery?

DONNA ANNA.
'Tis hard to know thy thoughts. How camest
                                        thou here?
Thou art in luck that none thy coming guessed;
For then thy death were certain and most sure.

DON JUAN.
And why fear death? To have a minute's sight
Of thee, I'll gladly give whole years of life!

DONNA ANNA.
But how succeed to get thee hence, madcap?

DON JUAN. (*Kissing her hand.*)
And thou art anxious for Don Juan's life?
I knew no hate could long a harbour find
In thy gracious breast, fair Donna Anna.

DONNA ANNA.

Ah, would to heaven I could but hate thee!
But 'tis already late, and we must part.

DON JUAN.

And when to meet again?

DONNA ANNA.

I do not know. :
Some future day.

DON JUAN.

To-morrow?

DONNA ANNA.

But where?

DON JUAN.

Here.

DONNA ANNA.

Ah, Don Juan, how weak I am of heart!

DON JUAN.

A cold kiss as earnest of our meeting!

DONNA ANNA.

Nay go, 'tis late!

DON JUAN.

One quiet kiss of peace!

DONNA ANNA.

Thou art importunate! Well, quick, take one!
(*A knock is heard.*)
What noise is that? Hide thyself Don Juan!

DON JUAN.

Farewell!... To our next meeting!... Darling friend!
(*Goes out, but immediately returns.*)
Ah!

DONNA ANNA.

What ails thee?... Ah!
(*The statue of the Commander appears. Donna Anna falls fainting.*)

STATUE.

At thy call I come.

DON JUAN.

Oh God! Donna Anna!

THE STATUE.

Approach her not!
It is all finished. Dost thou tremble, Don!

DON JUAN.

Not I... I called thee... am glad to see thee!

THE STATUE.

Give me thy hand.

DON JUAN.

    Oh, heavy is the grasp
Of his stone hand! Let go, let go my hand!
I die... it is the end... Donna Anna!

BORIS GODOUNOFF.

AN HISTORICAL TRAGEDY IN TWENTY FIVE SCENES.

BORIS GODOUNOFF.

SCENE THE FIRST.

(February 20. 1598.)

Rooms in the Kremlin Palace.

PRINCE SHOUISKY. PRINCE VOROTINSKY.

VOROTINSKY.

We have been ordered to patrol the streets,
In vain, it seems, for none are left to watch;
Deserted is the town, and all are gone
Together with the Patriarch to pray
In convent church: how will it end, thinkst thou?

SHOUISKY.

How will it end? It is not hard to guess:
The people will a little longer rave and weep,
Boris will yet grimace a little while,
As drunkards do before a cup of wine,
But in the end will graciously consent,
And with no more demur accept the crown:
And then... why, then he will begin to rule
Exactly as before he ruled.

VOROTINSKY.

A month
Has passed since he, renouncing worldly things,
The convent doors close shut upon himself
And sister. All this time, nor Patriarch
Nor Council of Boyards can turn his will.
He is untouched by tears, entreaties, prayers,
Or by the people's distraught cries of woe,
Nor does he heed the Great Assembly's vote.
In vain his sister have they humbly prayed
Boris to bless as future sovereign Tsar.
'Tis hard to move the haughty Nun-Tsaritza;
Like him she is firm; like him, inexorable;
Into her soul Boris has breathed his will.
And if the Regent should have weary grown
Of state affairs and all the cares they bring,
And mount the throne without the power to rule,
What wilt thou say?

SHOUISKY.

What shall I say? Why, this.
The blood of our Tsarevitch has flowed in vain;
And if this be the end, Dmitry might have lived.

VOROTINSKY.

A deed of blood-red horror! But is it true,
Boris the young Tsarevitch killed?

SHOUISKY.

Who else?
Pray, who but he sought Tcheptchougoff to bribe?
Who with Katchaloff sent in secret haste

The two Bietargovskys? I myself was sent
To Uglitch, that I might upon the spot
The crime and criminal unkennel quick;
And there I found clear proofs and traces fresh:
For all the town was witness of the deed,
And gave with one accord the story of the crime.
And when to Moscow I returned, one word
Had brought the murderer to open shame.

VOROTINSKY.

And wherefore didst thou not pronounce that word?

SHOUISKY.

I must confess, he made me doubt his guilt
By his assurance and his want of shame;
With honest glance he looked me in the eyes,
And asked that I would give details minute;
And I began repeat the fabled lies,
He cunningly himself suggested me.

VOROTINSKY.

Thy honour, prince?

SHOUISKY.

What wouldst thou have me do?
Discover all to Theodore? The Tsar
Looked only through the eyes of Godounoff,
Heard only through the ears of Godounoff.
Suppose, I had convinced him of my truth,
Boris would soon have unconvinced the Tsar,
And then and there have clapt me into jail,

And at the needful hour, my uncle's fate,
Would secret orders give to strangle me.
I will not boast, but, if occasion call,
No fate, however harsh, can keep me back;
I have no coward fear, but am no fool,
To thrust my head into the traitor's noose.

VOROTINSKY.

A foul and horrid deed! But it must be,
The murd'rer's soul is haunted with remorse;
Methinks, the body of the guiltless child
Must bar the path he treads to throne usurped.

SHOUISKY.

Across it he will stride: he knows not fear!
In truth, we Russians have great need to boast,
When he, the Tartar slave of yesterday,
Malouta's son-in-law, the kinsman near
Of hangman vile, hangman himself in soul,
Should take the crown and wear the purple robe!

VOROTINSKY.

He is low-born, we are of nobler rank.

SHOUISKY.

Well, so it seems.

VOROTINSKY.

Thy house and mine, thank God,
The whole world knows to be of princely race.

SHOUISKY.

The princely blood of Rurick flows in us.

VOROTINSKY.

But, listen, prince; we, then, should have the right
To follow Theodore.

SHOUISKY.

Yea, much more right
Than Godounoff.

VOROTINSKY.

'Tis plain.

SHOUISKY.

What should we do?
Boris will not give up his newest trick:
Let us be cunning, and the people stir
To cast aside their faith in Godounoff;
Princes enough they have from whom they can
Elect the one they would their ruler make.

VOROTINSKY.

No few of us can boast Varangan blood,
But hard the task to displace Godounoff!
The people are unused to see in us
The true descendants of their warlike chiefs.
The Princedoms we have long ago destroyed,
And long been vassal servants to the Tsars;
Whilst he has had the wit by fear and love
And fame to win the people to his side.

SHOUISKY.

Boris is bold... and that is all... whilst we...
Enough! For look, the people have come back;
Let us go forth, and his decision learn.

SCENE THE SECOND.

*The Red Square.
A Crowd of the People.*

ONE OF THE CROWD.

He is unmoved, and from his presence chased
The Bishops, and Boyards, and Patriarch.
In vain they lowly fell upon their knees,
He dreads the dazzling glory of a throne.

ANOTHER OF THE CROWD.

Alas, alas! Who, then, will deign to rule?
Woe is us!

A VOICE FROM THE CROWD.

The First Secretary, look,
Has come, and will the Council's vote announce.

THE PEOPLE.

Silence! The Secretary! Silence there!
Listen!

STCHELKALOFF.

(Speaking from the Red Steps).
It has in Council been resolved
Yet once again to prove the power of prayer

Upon the Regent's troubled, doubting soul.
To-morrow morn the Patriarch revered
Will solemn service in the Kremlin hold.
With banners hallowed and with image blest
Of Virgin of Vladimir and Donskoy,
By synod holy and Boyards attended,
With Council of the Nobles, legates chosen,
And sons of Moscow, thither will he go.
We all on knees shall pray the good Tsaritza
Pity take on wretched, orphaned Moscow,
And bless Boris as wearer of the crown.
And now, I bid you home in peace return,
To beg that, with God's grace, a nation's prayer
On swiftest wings to heaven may quickly mount!
         (The Crowd disperses).

SCENE THE THIRD.

*Before the Novodevitchy Monastery.
A Crowd of People.*

FIRST CITIZEN.

To the Tsaritza's cell they now have gone:
With them Boris, the Patriarch, and crowds
Of noblemen.

SECOND CITIZEN.

And what's the news?

FIRST CITIZEN.

The same:
In his refusal firm, but there is hope.

WOMAN. *(Carrying a child.)*

Don't cry, my pet, don't cry! The watchman there
Will come and take you if you cry, my pet!

FIRST CITIZEN.

What think you? Can we get beyond the bar?

SECOND CITIZEN.

Impossible! Why, here it is so close,
We cannot move, and farther on is worse.

The whole of Moscow has turned out. And look,
The ramparts, roofs, to highest belfry tower,
The very pinnacles and crosses too,
With faces are alive.

     FIRST CITIZEN.

  A splendid sight!

     SECOND CITIZEN.

What noise is that?

     FIRST CITIZEN.

    Listen! what cries are those?
The people groan and sob, their tears fast flow,
As down they fall upon the ground, like waves
Of standing corn that bend before the wind:
Well, mate, our turn has come, quick on our knees!

     PEOPLE.

Oh, pity us! Rule over us, and be
Our Tsar and Father!

     SECOND CITIZEN. *(In a low tone.)*
  Why all this weeping?

     FIRST CITIZEN.

What's that to us? The Boyards bid us weep:
'Tis not for us to reason!

     WOMAN.

    What say you?
We all are bid to weep? And you quite still, *(To child.)*

As if it naught concerned us? Here, watchman!
Now, weep, you brat? *(Child cries.)* That's good!

     FIRST CITIZEN.

         If all do weep,
We two must blub!

     SECOND CITIZEN.

       The tears refuse to come.
But what has happened?

     FIRST CITIZEN.

       Who is there can tell?

     PEOPLE.

He wears the crown! He's Tsar! He has agreed!
Boris is Tsar! Long life to our new Tsar!

SCENE THE FOURTH.

The Kremlin Palace.

BORIS. THE PATRIARCH. BOYARDS.

BORIS.

To thee, most holy Father, and to you,
Boyards, I have disclosed my inmost soul;
Yourselves know how I have the power supreme
With trembling fear and humbleness assumed;
So hard the post that fate reserves for me!
Fate calls me to succeed Ivan the Great,
Fate calls me to succeed the Angel-Tsar!
O spirit just, of sov'reigns father blest,
From thy high throne above behold thy slave,
Thy grace confer on him, whom thou didst love,
And whom with such rare honours thou didst load,
And give him strength to wield thy sacred sway!
Oh, may I rule my people to their glory,
Like thee, may I be ever true and just!
In this my work I pray your aid, Boyards,
Serve me as truly as you well served him,
When I your labours and your toils did share,
As yet unchosen by the people's will.

BOYARDS.

We swear that to our oaths we'll ne'er prove false.

BORIS.

Now, let us forth, and pray before the tombs
Of mighty Tsars whom Russia loves to greet:
Then will we meet and solemn banquet hold.
Our subjects all, both high and low, we bid;
To one and all we give our welcome free!
(The assembly breaks up, Vorotinsky joining Shouisky.)

VOROTINSKY.

Thou hast well guessed.

SHOUISKY.

     Guessed what?

VOROTINSKY.

     But yesterday,
Rememb'rest thou?

SHOUISKY.

    I know not what thou sayst.

VOROTINSKY.

Why, when the crowds were from the Convent
          trooping,
Thou saidst....

SHOUISKY

   The hour forbids such things recall:

I counsel you forget them too, while time
Allows. Besides, with cunning venomed speech
I would but try to probe thy inmost soul,
And slily ferret out thy secret thoughts.
But see, the people throng to greet the Tsar;
My absence may be noted, do me harm:
I think, I'll join the crowd.   *(Exit Shouisky.)*

VOROTINSKY.

A fawning slave!

SCENE THE FIFTH.

(1603).

Night. A Cell in Tchudoff Monastery.

FATHER PEAMEN. GRIGORY *(sleeping).*

PEAMEN. *(Writing: a lamp burning on his table.)*

And now but one last record still remains,
And then my chronicle is ended quite,
The task fulfilled that God imposed on me,
A sinner. Not in vain have I been called
The deeds of many years to celebrate,
And make the lore of books my chief delight.
In future days, some student brother-monk
Shall find this scroll, the earnest of my life,
And lighting up, as I am wont, his lamp,
Shake from its covers worn the gathered dust,
And copy fair my annals true and just,
That teach the faithful, who come after us,
The changeful story of their country's past,
Recall to them their Tsars, illustrious
In labours, glory, and the good they did.
And lead them pray the Christ to pardon grant
For their ill deeds and for their darker crimes.
In my old age I seem to live once more,

As days gone by again before me pass.
Is it, in truth, so long since they flowed by,
Full-surging, like an ocean-sea, with storms?
To me they now are still and voiceless all:
Few heroes past yet live within my mind,
Of their great words but few are fresh preserved;
The rest, a shadow, leaves no trace behind!
But dawn is near; the lamp begins burn pale;
And now but one last record still remains!

GRIGORY.

(Waking up from his sleep.)
Once more that dream! 'Tis very strange! Three
                                            times
The same accursèd dream!... And all the while,
Before his lamp the good old man doth sit
And write, nor once in sleep his eyelids close.
I love to gaze upon his tranquil face,
As, buried mind and soul in days gone by,
His chronicle he pens; and oft I fain
Would from his looks discern of what he writes:
Or of the gloomy Tartar stifling yoke,
Or of Ivan's dark reign of tortures harsh,
Or of the streets of Novgorod blood-stained,
Or of our native country's fame. In vain:
Nor on his forehead high, nor in his glance,
Can I e'er read his secret, hidden thoughts;
He ever wears that calm, majestic mien,
Like some official clerk in service old,
Who looks unmoved on innocence and guilt,
And good or ill indifferent regards,
Nor sign of pity or of anger shows.

PEAMEN.

Thou hast awaked, good brother mine?

GRIGORY.

Bless me,
Holy father.

PEAMEN.

The Lord abide with thee,
And bless thee day and night throughout thy life!

GRIGORY.

Whilst thou, all night a stranger to repose,
Didst write, my rest an evil dream, the false
Creation of our common foe, has troubled.
Methought, that up a steep ascent I climbed,
And reached a tower from whose lofty height
No larger Moscow seemed than anthill's mound;
Below, the people thronged the city-square,
And, upward gazing, laughed and jeered at me:
With shame possessed, and losing self-command,
I fell headlong, and with the shock awoke.
I thrice have dreamed the same accursèd dream.
Is it not strange?

PEAMEN.

The play of youthful blood,
Which can alone by prayer and fast be tamed,
So that thy sleep be blessed with lighter dreams.
In my old age, if I, against my will
Subdued by toil of long-continued work,
Neglect to pray God's blessing on the night,

My sleep with sinful visions is disturbed;
And I once more am guest at royster's feast,
Again take part in wild exploit of war,
Or share in maddest freak of youthful years.

GRIGORY.

In gay and active life thy youth was passed.
Before Kazan's strong towers hast thou fought,
And under Shouisky the foe repulsed,
Hast known the court and pomp of great Ivan:
In all hast been kind fortune's favourite!
Whilst I, a monk from boyish years, have known
Till now no other change save change of cell.
I ne'er have known the rush and noise of war,
At table of the Tsar have ne'er been called
To feast. I, too, like thee, when old age came,
Would have renounced the world, its pleasures vain,
Have ta'en the vow, and lived in monkish cell

PEAMEN.

Do not repine that in thy early years
Thou didst renounce this sinful world, or that
The Highest spared thee trials too severe.
Believe my words: From early years we are
By fame, by pomp, by woman's love enslaved.
Too long I lived, gay pleasures at my beck,
But truest happiness have only felt
Since hither I was called to serve the Lord.
Dost thou, my son, of Tsars with envy think?
No rule, save God's alone, can top their sway,
And none oppose their will. Yet what are they?
The golden crown weighs heavy on their brow,

And gladly would they change it for the cowl.
The Tsar Ivan long sought full peace of soul
In monkish work and holy convent toil.
The palace, filled of yore with fawning slaves,
Now seemed the calm retreat of prayerful men:
And courtiers proud gave place to humble folk;
The Tsar himself assumed the Prior's dress.
I saw him once, e'en here, in this same cell,...
Wherein then lived the holy martyr Cyril,
The saintliest of men; it was the time
When God revealed to me the nothingness
And vain deceit of worldly things.... I saw the Tsar,
Worn out with schemes of cruel punishments;
Deep lost in thought the dread Tsar sat with us,
As silent we before him trembling stood,
And then began converse in quiet tone, -
As thus the monks and Prior he bespake:
„My fathers, soon the wished-for day will dawn,
When hither I, salvation thirsting, come;
Thou, Nicodeme, thou, Serge, and Cyril, thou,
And all of you shall then receive my vow:
For I shall come, a sinner in despair,
And kneeling, holy father, at thy feet,
Shall don the robe of true religion's peace."
Thus, weeping, spake the dread and mighty Tsar,
From forth his lips the words flowed soft and sweet;
With his our tears we mingled, as we prayed
The God of Heaven with calm and love to fill
His suff'ring, tortured soul, by passion tossed.
Or shall I tell of Theodore, his son?
Upon his throne he oft would dream the life
Of tranquil monk were his. The chamber royal

He changed into a room of prayer, where cares
Of troubled state were weak his soul to vex;
And God was pleased, and blessed the Angel-Tsar,
And gave his kingdom peace, and kept it safe.
His hour of death was also strangely marked
By sign of wonder sent from heaven direct:
Beside his bed, though seen by none save him,
Appeared a form that bright in glory shone,
With whom the youthful Tsar began commune,
And called him by the name of Patriarch.
And we who stood around were seized with fear;
The Patriarch, we knew, was distant far,
Nor near the spot where lay the dying Tsar.
And as he breathed his last, the room was filled
With sweetest fragrance, and his face a-glow....
We ne'er shall look upon his like again!
O woe untold, and crown of horrors dread!
We banished God from out our hearts, and sinned:
We chose the slayer foul of our young Tsar
To sit upon his throne.

GRIGORY.

    I oft have wished
To question thee, my father, of the death
Of Dmitry the Tsarevitch. Wert thou not
At Uglitch then?

PEAMEN.

    Too well I know the tale!
God willed that I should see the evil deed,
The monstrous crime. I had received command
To go to Uglitch, where I came the night.
Next morn, at service hour, I hear the clang

Of bells that ring the tocsin of alarm;
Throughout the city all is noise and cries,
The palace is besieged with eager crowds.
I thither run, and, looking round, I see
Before me stretched young Dmitry's lifeless form,
With throat deep cut, and o'er her murdered child,
In deadly swoon, the pale Tsaritza falls,
Beside the corpse the foster-mother kneels.
Meanwhile, the people, mad with fury, hale
From place to place the nurse who traitress played.
And now appears before us, pale with fear,
Bietargovsky, the Judas butcher foul.
„See, see, the assassin!" shriek the maddened mob:
A minute more, and he has ceased to live.
The people rush to seek the murd'rers three,
In haste they seize the shrinking criminals,
And bring them close beside the child's cold corpse;
When, wonder-working heaven! the blood flows forth.
„Confess!" with one loud shout the people yell:
And, fearing death, the three confessed their crime,
And gave their hirer's name,... the name, Boris.

GRIGORY.

How old was then Dmitry the Tsarevitch?

PEAMEN.

His seventh year just passed: he now would be...
For this took place ten years ago.... nay, more,
Twelve years at least... in age the same as thou,
Had he but lived to reign... God's will be done!
It is with this sad story I conclude
The chronicle I write, for from that time

I mix but little with the outer world.
Grigory, listen, thou hast studied well,
Canst read and write, this charge bequeath I thee:
In hours free from work religious, write
With pen impartial all that thou mayst see;
Both wars and peace, the rule of sov'reign Tsars,
The mighty wonders wrought by God's elect,
The prophets and the signs from heaven sent.
The hour is late, I feel I need must rest,
And lamp I will extinguish now.... But hark,
The matin-bell... The Lord have mercy on
Us, his slaves! Give here my staff, Grigory!
(Exit Peamen.)

GRIGORY.

Boris! Boris! all quake before thee now!
Nor is there one who dares thy guilt denounce,
The bloody fate of thy young, stainless prey.
Meanwhile, the monk-recluse within his cell
Records in flaming words the horrid crime;
And, as God's judgment shall not ever sleep,
E'en so thou canst not hush man's sentence just.

SCENE THE SIXTH.

Within the enclosed grounds of the Monastery.

GRIGORY. A MONK.

GRIGORY.

How dull and weary is the course of our poor monkish life!
Day follows day: the same eternal things we see and hear:
See nothing but black copes, hear nothing but the chapel bell.
The whole day long we yawn and potter, doing naught the while;
The night disturbed with blackest thoughts and dreams of outer world;
That one is glad when bell strikes loud enough to wake the dead.
Within these close confines I can no longer live or breathe;
The world is wide: its many roads lie open to my choice,
I'll disappear, be lost, and counted dead!

MONK.

In truth, this life

Is dull and harsh for you warmblooded, hot, and lusty
youths!

GRIGORY.

If but the Khan would threat again, or Litva stir
revolt!
I then would go and gladly try my trusty sword with
them!
If but our good Tsarevitch could from his dark tomb
arise,
And cry aloud: „My children loyal, faithful, where
are ye?
Boris ye serve, and fight for him who slily worked
my ill;
Stand up against my foe, and hurl him to the shades
below!"

MONK.

Enough! Thou speakst but foolish, empty words.
The dead rise not.
Another fate, it seems, the young Tsarevitch was
decreed.
But hearken, if thou wouldst the scheme succeed,
then wisely scheme.

GRIGORY.

What dost thou mean?

MONK.

Were I but young and hale in years like thee,
And had not creeping age made silver gray my once
brown hairs,...
Thou knowst what I would say?

GRIGORY.

In riddles thou dost speak.

MONK.

Listen!
The common mob are fools, the dupes of any clever wight,
Most easily deceived, for ever seeking wonders new;
The Boyards, too, in Godounoff do but their equal own,
For even now the old Varangan race is dear to all.
In bearing, form, and years with the Tsarevitch thou art one,
And if thou courage hast.

GRIGORY.

I understand.

MONK.

Well, what sayst thou?

GRIGORY.

The die is cast! I am henceforth Dmitry, the Tsarevitch!

MONK.

And shalt be Tsar! In earnest pledge whereof give me thy hand.

SCENE THE SEVENTH.

The Patriarch's Palace.

THE PATRIARCH. THE PRIOR OF TCHUDOFF MONASTERY.

PATRIARCH.

And he has run away, Father Prior?

PRIOR.

My lord, three days ago he disappeared.

PATRIARCH.

A rogue accursed! And who is he by birth?

PRIOR.

He is of the family of the Otrepieffs, Boyards of Galitch. In his youth he became a monk, I know not where; later, he lived at Sousdal, in the Euphemia Monastery, which he soon left, and for a while wandered from place to place, till he came to Tchudoff, and joined our brotherhood. As he was still young and inexperienced, I placed him under the care of Peamen, an old man, gentle by nature and kind in character: and he gave himself up to study, read our old chronicles, composed canons to the glory of the saints; but his learning, it is plain, came not from God.

PATRIARCH.

Again, these men of learning! What vain things has he not imagined! „I shall be the Tsar of Moscow!" Alas, he is a vile vessel of wrath, reserved for eternal damnation! We must not let the Tsar know aught of this: it would only vex and trouble him. Enough, if we officially report his flight to one of the Secretaries, to Smirnoff or Eupheme. A damnable heresy, this: I shall be the Tsar of Moscow! He must be forthwith pursued and arrested, and then we will send him to Slovetsky, and keep him there in close confinement for life, that he may repent. For it is a devilish heresy; is it not, Father Prior?

PRIOR.

Heresy, my lord, rank heresy!

SCENE THE EIGHTH.

A Room in the Imperial Palace.

BORIS. TWO MEAT-BEARERS.

FIRST MEAT-BEARER.

Where is the Tsar?

SECOND MEAT-BEARER.

In his sleeping-chamber,
Shut up with some warlock, the doors close-locked.

FIRST MEAT-BEARER.

Just so: such folk alone he now receives,
Sly fortune-tellers, charmers, or warlocks.
Like pretty bride, the future he divines:
I fain would know the future he foresees.

SECOND MEAT-BEARER.

Wouldst know? Look, here he comes. Thou now
canst ask.

FIRST MEAT-BEARER.

His face is dark with gloom.

(*They go out.*)

BORIS.

                      I now have reached
My highest point, and have these six years ruled
In peace; but power has brought my soul no bliss.
As in our youth we love, and, thirsting, seek
The joys of love, but, once the minute's thirst
Is quenched, the heart grows cold, and love begins
To cloy, and soon we weary of its charms.
In vain the warlock flatters me with hope
Of years prolonged and power undisturbed;
Nor power nor life can longer give me joy:
Beforehand, here, I feel God's light'ning glance.
No happiness can visit me. I thought
To bring my people glory and content,
By lavish gifts to win their loyal love;
But I have long abandoned that vain hope.
The mob a living power will ever hate,
And for the dead alone reserve their hearts.
We are but fools to heed the people's praise,
Or take to heart their wail of discontent.
The curse of hunger fell upon our land;
The people groaned, and wept, and wrung their hands:
Bread-granaries I founded, among the poor
I showered gold as gifts, and gave them work:
And they returned my good with curses wild!
A raging fire their homes and courts destroyed;
Fresh dwellings, new and strong, I built for them,
And they declared their houses I had burned!
Such is the mob, and yet men seek their love!
In my own home I sought to find my joy,
The future of my daughter to secure;

The storm-god, death, her youthful lord laid low,
And busy rumour's evil tongue denounced
Me, me, the sorrowing, heart-broken sire,
As guilty of my daughter's widowhood.
I am the primal cause of all men's woe:
I Theodore did hurry to his end;
'Twas I did plot the Nun-Tsaritza's death;
And on my burdened shoulders lies the fault.
I feel too late that nothing can bring peace,
Amidst the cares and sorrows of the world,
Naught save the conscience pure and free of crime.
And this, if pure, will overcome the bad,
Victorious it proves o'er ill report;
Whilst if but one black spot its surface stain,
E'en though it be the fruit of chance contact,
Then all is ill: the soul with feverish pest
Is all consumed, the heart with poison filled,
Reproaches, loud as hammer's knock, confound
The ears, and all is sick, the head is dizzy,
The eyes bloodshot and dull; and one would fain
Escape: alas! there is nowhere to flee.
Yea, woe to him whose conscience is unclean!

SCENE THE NINTH.

A Tavern near the Lithuanian Frontier.

MISAEL AND VARLAAM, *dressed as friars.* GRIGORY OTREPIEFF, *in a layman's dress.* HOSTESS. TWO WATCHMEN.

HOSTESS.

What can I serve you with, my honest sirs?

VARLAAM.

With aught God sends us, hostess. Hast thou wine?

HOSTESS.

What think you, fathers? Straight I'll bring you some.
(Exit hostess.)

MISAEL. *(To Grigory.)*

Why, mate, art thou so fallen in the dumps? Here we are close to the Lithuanian frontier thou hast been so eager about.

GRIGORY.

Till I am in Lithuania, there is no quiet or repose for me.

VARLAAM.

What is the great charm that Lithuania has for thee? Now, father Misael and I, poor sinner, since we have hooked the monastery, do not bother our heads, whether we be in Lithuania or in Russia. Fiddle or psaltery, it is all the same to us, provided only the wine does not fail... Ah, here it comes.

MISAEL.

Admirably spoken, father Varlaam, and to the point.

HOSTESS. (*Coming into the room.*)

Here is the wine, my fathers. Drink, and health and good luck attend you!

MISAEL.

Thanks, my dear: may the Lord bless thee! (*They drink; Varlaam sings snatches from a song*). Why dost thou not join us in our song and drink?

GRIGORY.

I don't wish.

MISAEL.

Every one is free to do as he likes.

VARLAAM.

Ah, father Misael, it is only when in drink, a man knows the joys of Paradise! Let us drink to the health of our hostess. (*He drinks.*) Now, father Misael, when I am drinking, I hate your sober folk. You see, drinking, that's one thing, and sour prudery, that's another. Do you wish to jog with us, very pleased, if you will join; if not, get out, and the deuce take you. Jesters and priests never make good mates!

GRIGORY.

Drink, and lay down the law for thyself!... Thou seest,
I too, when it is necessary, can speak to the point!

VARLAAM.

And pray, why lay down a law for myself?

MISAEL.

Let him alone, and leave off bothering, father Varlaam!

VARLAAM.

Tell me, who is this drink-faster? He of his own accord joined our company, never once telling us who he is, or where he comes from. And now he begins to sermonise.

(*He drinks, and sings a song.*)

GRIGORY. *(To the hostess.)*

Where does this road lead to?

HOSTESS.

Into Lithuania, good friend, to the Louovie hills.

GRIGORY.

And is it far to the Louovie hills?

HOSTESS.

Not very far, thou canst easily get there by night fall, unless, by chance, thou art stopped at the gates, or by the watchmen, on the road.

GRIGORY.

How stopped? What dost thou mean?

HOSTESS.

There is a runaway from Moscow they are after, and orders have been given to stop and search all travellers.

GRIGORY. *(Aside.)*

A regular St. George's Day for me! *(Aloud.)* But who is it they are after? Who has run away from Moscow?

HOSTESS.

The Lord alone knows! some robber or brigand; at any rate, honest people can no longer travel freely. And what will come of it all? Nothing: they will never catch the poor devil. As if there were no other way into Lithuania, than by the highroad! Why, one has only to turn to the left, go through the pine-forest up to the chapel on the Tchekansky river, and then cut across the marsh to Chopino, and from thence to Zachereva, and from there any child can get to the Louovie hills. These blessed watchmen are only a burden to honest travellers, and we poor people are robbed on every side by the brutes. *(A noise is heard.)* What is that? Here are the cursed scoundrels! They have come to search the place.

GRIGORY.

Hostess, is there no corner in the house, where one can hide?

HOSTESS.

No, dear friend, I should only be too glad myself to hide somewhere. There is nothing to be done when they come, but to give them wine and bread, and God knows what else. I wish they would burst with their gorging!

(Enter two watchmen.)

WATCHMEN.

Good day, hostess!

HOSTESS.

Welcome, good friends! Please, come in.

SECOND WATCHMAN. *(To the first.)*

We are in luck to-day: a drinking bout is going on. *(To the monks.)* What people are you?

VARLAAM.

We are aged servants of the Lord, peaceable monks, on our way through the villages, to collect the alms of the faithful in aid of our monastery.

FIRST WATCHMAN. *(To Grigory.)*

And thou?

MISAEL.

Our companion...

GRIGORY.

A layman of the neighbouring town. I am their guide as far as the frontier, and there I must leave them and go home.

MISAEL.

What, hast thou changed thy mind?

GRIGORY. *(In a low tone.)*

Hush! be silent!

FIRST WATCHMAN.

Hostess, bring some more wine! We will have a drink and a chat with these monks.

SECOND WATCHMAN. *(In a low voice.)*

The younker does not seem to be very flush: there is nothing to be got out of him, but the old men...

FIRST WATCHMAN.

Keep quiet, we will soon ferret out all about them... Well, my fathers, and how is your business going?

VARLAAM.

Badly, my son, very badly. Times have changed; Christians have grown stingy, and become lovers of pelf and hoarders of money. They give but little to the Lord. The nations of the earth have fallen into sin; they have given themselves up to buying and selling; they think only of this world's goods, and have no care for their soul. We trudge and trudge, begging here and begging there, and at the end of three days have not made a half-copeck. A wicked world! One week goes by, a second and a third; and when at last we turn out the bag, there is so little in it, that we are ashamed to return to the monastery, and what is to be done? Out of very grief, we drink away the trumpery sum. We can't help ourselves! Yes, things go badly, and the last days have come upon us!

HOSTESS. *(Weeping.)*
The Lord have mercy on us and deliver us from evil!
(Whilst Varlaam is talking, the first watchman has kept his eyes fixed on Misael.)

FIRST WATCHMAN.
Alexis, you have the Imperial Decree?

SECOND WATCHMAN.
Yes, I have it here in my pocket.

FIRST WATCHMAN.
Give it me.

MISAEL.
Why dost thou look at me so fixedly?

FIRST WATCHMAN.
Why, you see, an evil-minded heretic, named

Grigory Otrepieff, has run away from Moscow. May be, thou hast heard about it?

MISAEL.

No, I have heard nothing of it.

FIRST WATCHMAN.

So, thou hast heard nothing of it? Very good! Now, this runaway heretic the Tsar has ordered to be arrested and hanged. You know that?

MISAEL.

No, no: I know nothing of the affair.

FIRST WATCHMAN. *(To Varlaam.)*

Canst thou read?

VARLAAM,

When I was young, I learned to read; but I have forgotten since.

FIRST WATCHMAN. *(To Misael.)*

And thou?

MISAEL.

The Lord has not given me that gift.

FIRST WATCHMAN.

Well, here is the Tsar's Decree.

MISAEL.

But what has it to do with me?

FIRST WATCHMAN.

It seems to me that this fugitive heretic, thief, and rogue is no other than thyself.

MISAEL.

Good God! What art thou saying?

FIRST WATCHMAN.

Wait a little! Shut to the doors! We'll soon get at the truth.

HOSTESS.

Ah, how they like to torture honest folk! they won't even let this poor man alone!

FIRST WATCHMAN.

Who is here able to read?

GRIGORY. *(Coming forward.)*
I can read and write.

FIRST WATCHMAN.

Indeed? And who taught thee?

GRIGORY.

Our sacristan.

FIRST WATCHMAN.

Well, read that out loud.

GRIGORY. *(Reading.)*

Grigory, an unworthy monk of Tchudoff Monastery, of the family of the Otrepieffs, has fallen into heresy, and with his devilish errors has sought to contaminate the holy brotherhood From information received, it appears that this accursed Grigory has fled to the borders of Lithuania...

FIRST WATCHMAN. *(To Misael.)*

And thou still affirmest, thou art not the man?

GRIGORY. *(Reading.)*

And the Tsar hereby orders him to be arrested...

FIRST WATCHMAN.

And to be hanged.

GRIGORY.

There is nothing here about hanging.

FIRST WATCHMAN.

Nonsense! Of course every word is not put down in full! So, please, read it properly and correctly: to be arrested and hanged.

GRIGORY. *(Reading.)*

And to be hanged. Grigory is about fifty years of age, of middle height, bald-headed, with a light gray beard, and a prominent belly.

(All turn their eyes on Varlaam.)

FIRST WATCHMAN.

Friends, that is Grigory! Seize him, and bind him! It has turned out differently to what I expected.

VARLAAM. *(Seizing the paper.)*

Hands off, you rogues! What kind of Grigory, pray, am I? How, fifty years of age, a gray beard, and a prominent belly! Nay, brother, thou art too young to trick me like that! I have got out of the way of reading, and can't very easily spell out the words; but when it comes to hanging, I can read fast enough. *(Reads with difficulty.)* This Grigory is about twenty years of age. Where is there a word about fifty? Canst thou not read, dear brother? Twenty!

SECOND WATCHMAN.

Yes, I recollect, it was twenty; that is what we were told.

FIRST WATCHMAN. *(To Grigory).*

How is this, friend? It seems, you are fond of playing a joke.
(All this while Grigory stands with his head low bent, and his hands crossed on his breast.)

VARLAAM. *(Continuing to read.)*

He is of short stature, with broad chest, one arm shorter than the other, blue eyes, reddish hair, a mole on his cheek, and another on his forehead... What dost thou say, friend; I fancy, thou art the man. *(Grigory suddenly pulls out a dagger; all give way before him, and he leaps through a window.)*

WATCHMAN.

Hold him! Hold him there!

SCENE THE TENTH.

Moscow, Shouisky's House.

SHOUISKY. POUSHKIN. GUESTS. A BOY.

SHOUISKY.

(All rising from their places.)
Give here more wine. And now, dear friends, we'll pledge
The last and crowning toast!
(To boy-chanter.)
Recite the prayer.

BOY.

O King of Heaven blest, that from all times
And in all places art, fulfil our prayer!
We humbly pray Thee for our Sov'reign dread,
Whom Thou hast called to be the Lord and Head
And Autocrat Supreme of Christian folk;
Beneath his palace roof, on battle field,
In journeys wide, or sleeping on his couch,
Protect and shield him with Thy helpful grace.
O'er all his foes make him victorious;
Extend his glory-fame from sea to sea.
With health and length of days his household bless;
Wide let his race o'er all the world be spread;

And may he show to us, his faithful slaves,
As ever he hath shown in days before,
Forbearance, pity, love, and patience.
And from his wisdom, that no limits bind,
As from rich source, may unstrained justice flow.
And raising high with loud acclaim the bowl,
We pray the King of Kings to bless our Tsar!

SHOUISKY. *(Drinking.)*

Long years and happy to our mighty Tsar!
I wish you all, dear friends, a kind farewell;
Accept my thanks that you have deigned to share
My bread and salt. Good slumbers wait you all!
(Exeunt guests, whom Shouisky accompanies to the door.)

POUSHKIN.

It is only by force thou hast got rid of them! To tell the truth, Prince Vassiely Ivanovitch, I began to fear, I should have no chance of a word with thee in private.

SHOUISKY. *(To the servants.)*

What are you standing there for with gaping mouths? Is it your place to hear what your masters have to say? Clear away the tables, and leave us alone.... What is it, Athanasius Michaelovitch?

POUSHKIN.

A marvel, and naught else! A courier
My nephew, Gabriel, from Kracoff sends.

SHOUISKY.

Well?

POUSHKIN.

Most strange the news my nephew writes:
Dread Ivan's son.... but stop!...
(Goes to door and carefully looks out.)
He whom Boris at Uglitch put to death....

SHOUISKY.

That is stale news, good prince.

POUSHKIN.

A minute wait:
The young Dmitry lives!

SHOUISKY.

That, indeed, is news!
The young Tsarevitch lives! A marvel, true,
But, as thou saidst, nothing more.

POUSHKIN.

Listen yet:
Whoe'er he be, young Dmitry saved from death,
Or spirit that his image has assumed,
Or reckless, daring rogue, pretender false,
This, at least, is sure: Dmitry has appeared.

SHOUISKY.

It cannot be.

POUSHKIN.

Poushkin himself was there,
And saw how he first time to palace came,
And through the rangèd lines of nobles passed,
And to the King's own private room made way.

SHOUISKY.

But who is he, and whence comes he?

POUSHKIN.

None know;
'Tis only known, he served awhile as slave
In Visnevetsky's house, where he fell ill,
And told his priest the secret of his birth.
The haughty Pole, of this informed, at once
The sick man sought, and nursed him in his bed,
And then set off with him to Sigismund.

SHOUISKY.

And what report give men of this smart sprig?

POUSHKIN.

They say he is wise, and affable, and sly;
Beloved by all. The Moscow runaways
He has securely won. The Latin priests
Are on his side. The King does flatter him,
And, it is said, his active aid has sworn.

SHOUISKY.

All this, dear friend, is turmoil so confused,
To make a poor man's puzzled head turn round.
He is, no doubt, a cheat that plays on men,
But, I confess, great danger lies a-head:
The news is grave, and should the people come
To know of it, a storm will burst on us!

POUSHKIN.

And such a storm, that Tsar Boris will find
It hard to keep the crown on his sly head;
And he will reap what he has sown. He rules,

As Tsar Ivan:... ill dreams be far from us!...
What gain, if open punishments have ceased,
If we no longer on the bloody pale
Before the mob commend our souls to Christ;
If now we are not burned upon the square,
And he no more with staff the ashes rakes?
Are our poor lives one whit the surer made?
Each one of us, we live beneath the fear
Of ban, exile, the prison, cowl, or chains,
Or death from hunger in the wilds, or noose.
Where are the noblest heroes of our race?
Where are prince Schietsky, or prince Schistounoff,
Romanoff, once our fallen country's hope?
Imprisoned close, or doomed to cruel death.
In time, such too will be thy certain fate!
Ourselves the victims of a lot as hard;
At home surrounded by unfaithful slaves,
And not a tongue but ready to betray,
No man but he and his have bought and bribed.
Our lives, our all, depend upon the first
Rude hind, whose provèd crimes we dare chastise.
And now, he has Saint George's day suppressed;
No longer have we power on our domains:
„The idle serf discharge not. Pleased, or not,
Both feed and nourish him. Nor shalt thou change
Thy workmen-slaves". Such is his new decree.
Beneath the iron rule of Tsar Ivan,
Such patent, flagrant wrong was never known.
The people ask, if they are now content:
And let this new Pretender try his luck,
And promise them once more Saint George's Day,
The game is his.

SHOUISKY.

Thou speakst the truth, good friend;
And yet, methinks, of this and much akin,
We will awhile strict silence keep.

POUSHKIN.

Of course,
We each for his own skin must care. But thou
Art wise, and much I like to chat with thee.
This news has deeply stirred me to my soul,
I could not help my fears with thee to share;
Besides, the truth to tell, thy wine and beer
Have made me indiscreet of speech to-day.
Farewell, good Prince.

SHOUISKY.

Till our next meeting, friend!

SCENE THE ELEVENTH.

Interior of the Kremlin Palace.

THE TSAR. THE TSAREVITCH. *(Drawing a map.)*
THE TSAREVNA. THE TSAREVNA'S NURSE. SIMON GODOUNOFF.
SHOUISKY.

KSENIA. *(Kissing a portrait.)*

My darling bridegroom, noble prince, not to me, thy bride, wert thou fated to belong, but to a dreary grave in a foreign land! Never shall I know peace again, but will ever mourn and weep for thee!

NURSE.

Ah, Tsarevna, a maiden weeps as easily as the dew falls; the sun comes out, and the dew is quickly dried. Another lord, fair and gracious, will come to woo thee, and thou, darling of our eyes, wilt love him, and wilt forget Prince Johann.

KSENIA.

Nay, nurse, nay. I shall ever remain faithful to the dead.

(Enters Boris.)

THE TSAR.

How now, Ksenia, how, my darling child?
Thou art in bridal years a widow made,
The bridegroom's death dost ever weep and mourn.
Alas, my child, the jealous fates denied
That I should be the maker of thy bliss.
Perchance, for some offence against dear God,
I might not rear with love thy future weal:
But why the innocent be doomed to weep?...
And thou, my son, art busy? What is that?

THEODORE.

A map of Muscovy, our wide domains
In all their vast extent. Look, Moscow here,
Here Novgorod, here Astrachan, and here
The sea, and dense, unwinsome woods of Perm,
And here Siberia.

THE TSAR.

    And what denotes
This winding line?

THEODORE.

    That line the Volga marks.

THE TSAR.

'Tis well. How sweet the fruit of learning is!
As from a point in heaven, we can scan
The whole empire, its borders, rivers, towns.
Be diligent, my son, for science gives
The slow results of swiftly flowing life.
The hour will come, and may be soon, when all

These regions wide, which thou, with finger deft,
Hast here on paper traced, shall fall beneath
Thy sway, and gladly own thee as their Tsar.
Be diligent, my son; the cares of rule
Shall thus be made the lighter and more clear.
       (Enters Simon Godounoff)
Here comes good Godounoff, with his reports.
Ksenia, leave us and go into thy room!
Farewell, my child, the Lord abide with thee!
       (Exeunt Ksenia and the Nurse.)
And now, what news, Simon, most trusty friend?

SIMON GODOUNOFF.

To-day, at dawn, Vassiely's steward came,
As well as Poushkin's servants, with reports.

THE TSAR.

What else?

SIMON GODOUNOFF.

From them I learned that yestermorn
Some messengers from Kracoff he received,
Who back returned in haste an hour later.

THE TSAR.

They have been seized?

SIMON GODOUNOFF.

Our men are on their track.

THE TSAR.

And what of Shouisky?

SIMON GODOUNOFF.

       Last night, among
Some other guests the Mieloslavskies came,
Young Saltikoff, Poushkin, and Butterlien.
They broke up late. But Poushkin stayed behind,
Was closeted alone with his sly host,
And they did long and earnest converse hold.

THE TSAR.

Bid hither Shouisky at once.

SIMON GODOUNOFF.

         My sire,
He is already here.

THE TSAR.

    Then, I will see him.
(Exit Simon.)

THE TSAR.

With Litva leagued! What means this friendship
            new?
The Poushkin house has ever been hostile,
Nor can I place my trust in Shouisky,
A shuffling, cunning rogue, but bold and false!
      (Enters Shouisky.)
Myself I wished to speak with thee, good prince,
But, as it seems, thou wert already here;
And I would first hear what thou hast to say.

SHOUISKY.

My sire, it is my duty to impart
Intelligence most strange.

THE TSAR.

I pray, say on.

SHOUISKY. *(Pointing to Theodore.)*

But sire...

THE TSAR.

Methinks, the prince, my son, may hear
All that a Shouisky can know. Speak on.

SHOUISKY.

From Lithuania the news has come...

THE TSAR.

But say, dear prince, is not thy news the same
As that which Poushkin yesterday received?

SHOUISKY. *(Aside.)*

We are betrayed... I had believed, my sire, *(Aloud.)*
The secret was as yet unknown to thee.

THE TSAR.

It matters not, good prince. I would compare
Thy news with mine, or else it will be hard
The truth to learn.

SHOUISKY.

I only know, a false
Pretender has late in Kracoff risen,
The King and nobles have declared for him.

THE TSAR.

And who may this new-fledged Pretender be?

SHOUISKY.

I cannot learn.

THE TSAR.

Where, then, the danger, prince?

SHOUISKY.

Without dispute, thy might is powerful;
Thy clemency, munificence, and zeal
The hearts of all thy slaves have fast enchained.
But, as thou knowest well, the stupid mob
Is fickle, mutinous, and easy gulled,
The victim light of each vain tale and hope,
The passing moment's easy, willing dupe,
To truth all deaf, indifferent to right,
The greedy picker-up of fabled lies.
The shameless quack can count upon their grace;
And should this paltry beggar's son succeed
To slip our watch and cross the borderland,
At once a crowd of gaping partisans
Will flock and hail the risen prince, Dmitry.

THE TSAR.

Dmitry!... how so?... what dost thou say?... that boy!...
Dmitry!... Tsarevitch,, go!... Quickly leave us!

SHOUISKY. *(Aside.)*

He reddens and the storm will soon burst forth!

THEODORE.

Thou wilt permit, my sire?

THE TSAR.

I cannot; go!
(Exit Theodore.)

Dmitry!

SHOUISKY. *(Aside.)*

I see, 'tis well, he nothing knows!

THE TSAR.

Listen, prince! Without delay fit measures take,
That Russia be from Litva close cut off
By serried lines of close ranged troops, and see
No soul the boundary doth cross, nor hare
From Poland hither scud, nor crow be let
From Kracoff fly. I charge thee, see to it.

SHOUISKY.

I go.

THE TSAR.

But stay! Thinkst not, this news of thine
Our langhter should provoke! Was ever time,
The buried dead were known to quit their graves,
And question with the Tsar, the lawful Tsar,
By all the people chosen as their prince,
With holy oil anointed by the church;
Must this, I ask, not move our mirth?... Well, what?
Say, why thou dost not laugh?

SHOUISKY.

I, sire?

THE TSAR.

                                  Listen,
Vassiely, my dear prince! When first I learned
News of this boy's... that he had strangely died,
By means unknown and long before his time,
Then thou wert sent to make enquiries. Now,
By God's most holy name and by the cross,
I charge thee tell the truth, and say, if thou
Didst plainly recognise the murdered boy,
And if there was no juggling trick? Reply!

SHOUISKY.

  I swear to thee...

THE TSAR.

                    Nay, Shouisky, swear not:
But say, it was the dead Tsarevitch?

SHOUISKY.

                                  He!

THE TSAR.

  Bethink thee, prince. I pardon promise thee,
Nor will I for thy former lie decree
Exile or other pain. But if to-day
Thou darest to trick me, then, by my son's head
I swear, a doom shall quickly visit thee,
Such doom, that Tsar Ivan himself shall turn
And quake with horror in his gloomy grave.

SHOUISKY.

  No punishment, save thy displeasure dread,
I fear, nor dare I now before thee lie.

It cannot be I was so blind as not
To recognise the young Dmitry. Three days
I saw his body in cathedral laid,
And thither flocked in crowds the Uglitch folk.
Around him lay the thirteen bodies dead
Of those the maddened mob to pieces tore.
With them decay had now its work begun,
Whilst still the prince's face was clear and fresh,
And smiling as in sleep that knows no care;
The ugly, gaping wound had yet not closed,
And save for that he bore no signs of death.
Nay, sire, there is no place for doubt. Dmitry
Sleeps in his grave.

            THE TSAR.
            Enough! You may depart.
                    (*Exit Shouisky.*)
'Twas hard to bear!... But now, I breathe again!
The while he spake, I felt the tingling blood
Suffuse my face and leave it then all pale.
For thirteen years that one and same sad shape,
That murdered child, has closely haunted me:
Yes, yes, it must be so; I understand.
But what is he, this threat'ning foe of mine?
What can he be to me? A shadow's name!
Can, then, a shadow don my royal robes,
A name my sons rob of their lawful rights?
Why, what a fool am I! There's naught to fear!
Blow but a breath, the phantom is dislimned!
And so, I am resolved; henceforth, no fear;
But naught must be unheeded or despised:...
Uneasy weighs the crown of Monomach!

SCENE THE TWELFTH.

Kracoff. Visnevetsky's House.

THE PRETENDER. FATHER TCHERNIKOFFSKY. POUSHKIN. KOURBSKY. CHOUSTCHOFF. AND OTHERS.

THE PRETENDER.

Nay, father mine, count not our task so hard;
Full well I know my people's spirit true;
In their religion free from rude excess,
With them the Tsar is sole exemplar guide.
Indifference is mark of tolerance.
I warrant, ere two years have passed away,
My people and the Eastern Church will own
The rule supreme of Peter's holy chair.

FATHER TCHERNIKOFFSKY.

May Saint Ignatius be thy surest aid,
When these new days shall happily arrive.
Meanwhile, these seeds that have by heaven's grace
Been sown, within thy heart, Tsarevitch, hide.
At times, our soul's high interests demand
That we should feign, and cheat the Gentile world:
Thy words and acts the world can rightly judge;
Thy thoughts and aim alone can God behold.

THE PRETENDER.

Amen!... Who knocks?... We will receive them straight.
(Enter many Russians and Poles).
To-morrow morn, my friends, we think to quit
This town. Three days I hope to spend, Mniszeck,
With thee as guest. Thy castle at Sambore,
Where welcome warm, I know, awaits thy Tsar,
For knightly pomp is famed throughout our land,
But chiefly famed for its young mistress fair,
Marina, whom I long to meet once more.
And you, my friends of Russia and brave Poles,
Who have, in closest brotherhood conjoined,
Your friendly banners raised on high against
The common foe, my enemy accursed;
You sons of Slavs, I soon shall lead your troops,
That long have yearned to strike the final blow....
Methinks, new faces here I do discern.

POUSHKIN.

They come to win thy gracious favour, sire,
And serve thee with their swords.

THE PRETENDER.

          Right welcome, friends!
But tell me, Poushkin, who that warrior
May be?

POUSHKIN.

'Tis Prince Kourbsky.

THE PRETENDER.

          A far-famed name!
The hero of Kazan thy kinsman was?

KOURBSKY.

I am his son.

THE PRETENDER.

He lives?

KOURBSKY.

Nay, he is dead.

THE PRETENDER.

He was alike in war and council great:
But since the famous day when he appeared
Before the ancient walls of Olga's city,
To take revenge on his despoilers proud,
Has naught been heard of him.

KOURBSKY.

My father, sire,
His latter years in Volhynia spent,
On lands the King of Poland granted him.
And there, from noise of life's turmoil removed,
His solace sought in learning and in books;
But peaceful studies brought nor joy nor peace,
He ne'er forgot the country of his youth,
But for the land that gave him birth he pined.

THE PRETENDER.

Alas, in what a flood of glory rose
The early morn of his tempestuous life!
But I am pleased to know, most noble knight,
His sons will with their King this day make peace.
'Tis well the sins of their sire to forget:

Peace to his grave! Approach, good friend.... thy hand!
But strange it is, a Kourbsky's son should place
Upon his throne the son of Tsar Ivan!
But all works well for me, both men and fate....
And thou?

     A POLE.

  A noble free, Sobansky named.

     THE PRETENDER.

Be thine all praise and honour, freedom's child!
At once one third give of his monthly pay....
What men are these? I see they wear the dress
Of our dear native land. They should be ours.

     CHROUSTCHOFF.

       (Bowing to the ground.)
  Our services accept, most sov'reign sire,
We are thy zealous slaves, who in disgrace
Have fled from Moscow, and are hither come
To greet our Tsar, and for thee are ready
Our lives to sacrifice, our bodies make
Sure steps whereby thou mayst ascend thy throne.

     THE PRETENDER.

You have long suffered blameless, but take heart!
Let me but make my way to Moscow's walls,
Boris shall well redeem your cruel wrongs....
And who art thou?

     CARELA.

    A Cossack from the Don.
The troopers free, their Hetmans bold and brave,

Both of the higher and the lower lands,
Have eyes to see and know their lawful Tsar,
And with their greetings loyal bid thee hail.

THE PRETENDER.

I know the people of the Don, and see
Their standards floating high with ours.
We thank our faithful soldiers of the Don:
Too well we know they have been robbed of all
Their dearest rights, oppressed, in bondage held.
Should God restore us to our father's throne,
We will bring back the ancient laws, and guard
The rights of our brave troopers of the Don.

POET.

*(Approaching with a low bow, and touching the hem
of the Pretender's robe.)*
Dread Prince of Sov'reigns most Serene and High!

THE PRETENDER.

What is thy prayer?

POET. *(Presenting a Paper.)*
That thou wouldst deign receive
This fruit unworthy of my loyal zeal.

THE PRETENDER.

And what is this I see? Choice Latin verse!
The tie is blest that binds the sword and lyre,
The consecrating laurel crowns them both.
Though I was born beneath a Northern sky,

I am no stranger to the Latin Muse,
And flowers love that on Parnassus grow,
And ne'er have lost my faith in poet's voice.
'Tis not in vain his fervent heart doth glow
With fire prophetic; his the gift supreme,
To bless and to foretell the hero's fame.
Come nearer, friend, and in remembrance take
This gift.   (*Giving him a ring.*)
        And when my fate has been fulfilled,
And I once more my crown ancestral wear,
Again I hope to hear thy dulcet voice,
And listen to thy lofty hymn inspired.
Musa gloriam coronat, gloriaque musam....
Farewell, my friends, to-morrow morn we meet.

ALL.

To arms, to arms! All hail, our Tsar, Dmitry!
All hail, our Tsar and Prince of Moscow dread!

SCENE THE THIRTEENTH.

Castle of the Governor Mniszeck at Sambore. Marina's Dressing-Room.

MARINA. ROUZA, *superintending her toilet.* A SERVANT.

MARINA. (*Looking in a glass.*)
How slow thou art! More haste, I pray, Rouza!

ROUZA.
A toilet you have chosen hard to range;
Which will you wear, the thread of sparkling pears,
Or emerald half-moon?

MARINA.
My diamond crown.

ROUZA.
That crown you wore, if I remember right,
When you were first presented at the court;
And at the ball, they say, outshone them all:
The men went mad, the women jealous chafed;
'Twas then the young Chotkevitch saw you first,
And later in despair destroyed himself.
What people say is true, one single glance
Will make a man a victim to your charms.

MARINA.

I pray you, quickly end.

ROUZA.

A minute more!
To-day your father builds his hopes on you:
'Tis known, your beauty the Tsarevitch struck,
Nor can he hide his love and passion deep:
He is a wounded bird, it now remains
For you to crown the blow, and net him safe.
For, Panna, he abandons all for you,
Pursues no more his warlike schemes, but since
He Kracoff left, the precious hours lets slip.
The battle field, the Moscow throne, are all
Forgot, and, while in love he suns himself,
Has lost the trust of Russian and of Pole.
Oh God, I scarce can wait the happy day!
But tell me once again that, when Dmitry
His fair Tsaritza into Moscow leads,
You will your faithful Rouza not forget.

MARINA.

And thinkst thou that I shall Tsaritza be?

ROUZA.

And who, save you? Which of our beauties here
Can hope to rival with my mistress fair?
To none your noble house need homage pay;
For mind and wit you are above compare...
And he is blest who wins your word or look,
And makes your maiden heart to beat with love,
Whoe'er he be, and though he were our King,

Or e'en the gallant Dauphin of gay France....
Not only is this Prince a beggar born,
The Lord alone knows who, or whence, he is!

MARINA.

The Tsar's true son, by all the world confessed.

ROUZA.

And yet, he served as slave last winter's months,
As we all know, in Visnevetsky's house.

MARINA.

He was in hiding there.

ROUZA.

              That too we know;
But have you heard the rumour spread abroad,
And what the common people say of him?
That he a chanter was, who Moscow fled,
When caught in some low knavish act of theft.

MARINA.

What folly!

ROUZA.

       I do not believe the tale!
I only say, he may regard himself
By fortune blest and highly favoured, if
You deign prefer his suit.

SERVANT. *(Entering)*,

          The guests are met.

MARINA.

You see, the whole night long you lose and waste
In idle chattering and gossip rude,
And I, meanwhile, cannot present myself.

ROUZA.

Now all is done.

MARINA. *(To herself.)*
The truth I'll make him tell.

SCENE THE FOURTEENTH.

A Suite of brilliantly lighted Rooms. Music.

VISNEVETSKY. MNISZECK. GUESTS.

MNISZECK.

With my Marina only does he speak,
It is to her alone he pays his court;
And all a happy ending doth forebode.
Now, Visnevetsky, say, didst thou e'er think
My daughter would one day Tsaritza be?

VISNEVETSKY.

A wondrous chance! Mniszeck, didst thou once
    think,
My common slave would mount the Moscow throne?

MNISZECK.

But own, the tact and skill my daughter shows!
I did but whisper in her ear: „Take heed,
And let not Dmitry through the fingers slip!"
And, lo, 'tis done, well caught and captured safe!
*(Music plays a polonaise. The Pretender and Marina
form the first couple.)*

MARINA.

(In a low voice to Grigory.)
To-morrow eve, an hour before midnight,
Near fountain in the avenue we meet.
(They pass on. Another Couple.)

CAVALIER.

But, pray, what finds he in her?

LADY.

Well, confess
She is a beauty.

CAVALIER.

Like a marble nymph,
With eyes that gleam not, lips that have no smile.
(A fresh couple.)

LADY.

Not handsome, but he has a pleasing look,
Besides, he wears the true imperial air.
(Another couple.)

LADY.

When do they march?

CAVALIER.

When the Tsarevitch wills.
We long are ready, but the fair Mniszeck
Both us and Dmitry keeps close captives here.

LADY.

A lot that most would share.

CAVALIER.

If only you....
(*They pass on. Rooms begin to empty.*)

MNISZEK.

We now are old, no longer care to dance,
And music gay has lost its witching charm,
Have ceased to press, or fondly kiss, fair hands:
And yet the freaks of youth are not forgot!
The world, methinks, is no more what it was:
Our youths have lost the knightly bearing bold,
Our beauties have become demurely cold,
And all, you must confess, is dull and dead.
So let us leave and go, dear friend, and bid
Uncork a bottle of our oldest wine,
Some cosy corner choose, where we may sit,
Enjoy its crusted fragrance, thick and ripe,
Whilst we discuss grave matter of import.
Away!

VISNEVETSKY.

And much there is we should debate.

SCENE THE FIFTEENTH.

Night. A Garden with Fountain.

THE PRETENDER. MARINA.

THE PRETENDER.

This is the fountain: hither she will come.
It is not nature makes me fearsome now:
Face to face I have stood with threat'ning death,
And death had not the strength to fright my soul.
Imprisonment for life did menace me,
I was pursued, but ne'er my spirit failed,
And boldness saved me from the prison-cell.
But now, my breath comes strangely thick and hard.
What mean this beating heart, these trembling limbs?
Is it the shudder of intense desire?
Not so: 'tis fear. The whole day long I wait
With eager hope the secret trysting-hour;
Thought over all that I have longed to say,
Planned how I best could bend her haughty will,
Kneeling, hail her with the name, Tsaritza.
But now the hour has come, forgotten quite
Are all the speeches I had learned by rote,
And tricksy love plays havoc with my brain...
But hearken, something glitters, something moves!

'Tis nothing but the cold moon's cheating light,
Murmur soft of evening breeze.

MARINA.

Tsarevitch!

THE PRETENDER.

'Tis she! My curdled blood has ceased to flow!

MARINA.

Dmitry! It is you?

THE PRETENDER.

Sweet, enchanting voice!
And art thou come at last? See I thee here,
Alone with me beneath the shades of night?
How slowly have the halting hours gone by,
Till dull-paced twilight melted into night!
How long I wait in darkness and in gloom!

MARINA.

The hours fly, and time to me is precious.
I have not thought to ask thee meet me here,
To listen to a lover's speeches soft.
We need no words to tell our love. I know
Thou lovest me. But learn, I am resolved
With thy fate, though stormy and uncertain,
Mine own to knit. And this, my firm resolve,
Gives me the right to ask one thing, Dmitry,
That thou to me discover now, at once,
Thy secret hopes, designs, and hardy schemes;
That I may, hand in hand, along the path

Of life thy equal tread, not led like child,
Nor as a slave to husband's light desires,
Nor be thy dumb, submissive concubine;
But as thy wife and spouse, the worthy peer,
And aid, and counsellor of Moscow's Tsar.

THE PRETENDER.

We will forget, if but for one bare hour,
The sordid cares and aching fears of fate;
Thyself forget that I Tsarevitch am!
But, rather, see in me the lover thou
Hast chosen of thy free, unfettered will,
Who lives but in the sunshine of thine eyes!
Oh, listen to the prayer of earnest love,
And let my heart give voice to all its plaint!

MARINA.

'Tis no fit time, my Prince. Thou idlest here,
Thy truest followers meanwhile wax cold;
From hour to hour the dangers and hardships
Grow still more dangerous and still more hard;
Vague rumours are already spread abroad.
And each new tale gives place to one more strange,
And Godounoff will slily hatch fresh plots.

THE PRETENDER.

Why speak of Godounoff? Does, then, thy love,
My soul's sole joy, on his proud will depend?
Nay, nay! With eyes of cold indifference
I now regard his throne and sov'reign power.
Thy love... of that deprived, life has no worth,
Nor glory's blaze, nor rule of Russian realm.

There on the steppe, in some rude hut of mud,
Thou shalt repay the loss of brightest crown;
Thy love...

MARINA.

Shame not thyself! Canst thou forget
The high and sacred call thou hast received?
To thee thy princely rank should dearer be
Than all the noisy, tinsel joys of life;
Naught else should hold a place within thy heart.
Not to the stripling, with his frothy vows,
Who will consent to be my beauty's slave,
But to the rightful heir of Moscow's throne,
To the Tsarevitch, saved by hand of fate,
To him I give with pride my heart and love.

THE PRETENDER.

Torment me not, Marina, I implore,
Nor say, that 'tis my rank, and not myself,
Has won thee. Nay, Marina, thou knowst not,
How, like a deadly drug, thy words my heart
Have poisoned... Can it be?... O horrid thought!..
But say, had chance refused me royal birth,
And were I not, in truth, great Ivan's son,
The boy, whom all the world has long forgot,
Wouldst thou, then, love me, as thou lovest now?

MARINA.

Thou canst not be another than thou art,
Nor could I other love.

THE PRETENDER.

                    No more, enough,
With a dead man I'll ne'er consent to share

His mistress-love, who still belongs to him;
Nor will I longer play a part. The truth
I'll tell, and thou shalt know that thy Dmitry
Lies in his grave, whence he can come no more.
And wouldst thou know who, then, I really am?
Well, if thou wouldst, learn this: I am a monk,
Who of his monkish dress and prison tired,
Beneath whose cowl a daring scheme was born,
A scheme to startle and convulse the world.
At last, the moment came. I fled my cell,
The Ukraine reached, found refuge in its huts,
Learned well to ride the steed and wield the sword,
Appeared to you, and Dmitry called myself.
Nor was it hard to cheat the brainless Poles.
And now, what will the proud Marina say?
Art pleased to know the secret of my soul?
What means this silence strange?

MARINA.

Oh, woe is me!

THE PRETENDER. *(Aside.)*

Alas, my fit of boyish discontent
In one short moment, it may be, has spoiled
Those future hopes I schemed with patient toil:
What have I thoughtless done?   *(To Marina)*
I see too well
None but a prince need hope to win thy hand.
I pray thee, quick pronounce the fatal word,
Thou art the sov'reign mistress of my fate:
Pronounce! Thy sentence, kneeling, I await.
(Kneels before her.)

MARINA.

Arise, pretender base and little-souled!
Thinkst thou, with worship of the bended knee
To charm, as though I had the easy heart
Of some weak girl, whom even thou canst gull?
Thou art deceived, my friend. At my feet I've seen
The courtliest of knights and lords high-named;
And if all coldly I repelled their suit,
'Twas not, in sooth, to please a beggar-monk.

THE PRETENDER. *(Rising up.)*

Do not, I pray, the young pretender scorn,
Whose heart, believe me, with a courage beats
That gives him right to sit on Moscow's throne,
And makes him worthy suitor of thy hand....

MARINA.

Or worthy of the hangman's rope, bold youth!

THE PRETENDER.

My crime I own. With proud ambition drunk,
I lied before my God, before His Tsar,
Before the world. But 'tis not thine, I feel
To punish me: to thee I have been true.
The world I could deceive, but never thee;
For thou hast ever been my angel-saint,
Before whose shrine I dare not lie or cheat.
Mad love, the jealous love that makes men blind,
And naught but love has forced me to disclose
My soul to thee.

MARINA.

And what hast thou to boast?

Who asked from thee confession of thy crime?
Methinks, if thou, a nameless, vagrant rogue,
Couldst with thy juggling cheat two peoples blind,
Thou shouldst have proved deserving of success,
And in thy heart of hearts have stubborn kept
Thy lie a hidden secret from the world.
And can I give my hand to one like thee?
Can I betray my kin and maiden shame,
And join my fate to thine, when thou thyself,
With low simplicity, blown by the wind,
Hast public made thy full and còmplete shame?
And he dare prate of love... from love he spake!
I marvel that, by friendship's claim impelled,
Thou hast not made my sire thy confidant,
Or with light heart revealed it to our King,
Or shown, at least, the true slave's faithful zeal,
And told Pan Visnevetsky all thy tale!

THE PRETENDER.

I swear that thou alone hast had the force
To wring from me the secret of my life.
I swear, that in no place and at no time,
At banquet, or at noisy drunken rouse,
Or in deep confidence with comrade sworn,
Or under threat of death, or torturing wheel,
Shall tongue of mine betray my burdened soul.

MARINA.

Thou swearst? And must I, therefore, need believe?
But why believe? By whom, I fain would know,
Wilt thou think well to swear? Perchance, by God,
Like novice when he takes his Order's oath?
Or by thy honour, like some errant Knight?

Or wilt thou, rather, as Tsarevitch swear
Upon thy word? Which oath best pleases? Speak!

THE PRETENDER.

The shade of Ivan has adopted me,
And from his grave the name Dmitry given,
Around me in revolt the people raised,
And doomed Boris to punishment condign.
I am Tsarevitch. But enough! I blush,
That I have cringed before a Polish girl.
Farewell! The chances of this bloody war,
The heavy cares imposed on me by fate,
Will smother soon, I ween, the pangs of love.
And when my passion's fever hot has cooled,
My love for thee shall turn to bitter hate
And now, I go. The victor's wreath or crown
Of thorns shall mark my triumph or disgrace;
On battle-field the hero's death I seek,
Or perish on the block in city-square.
But thou wilt not be near to joy or grieve,
But thou wilt not be near to share my fate;
And yet, methinks, too late thou shalt regret
The lot thou hast behind thee cast with scorn.

MARINA.

But what, if I should publish to the world
The story of thy bold and shameless cheat?

THE PRETENDER.

Thinkst thou, I need to fear what thou canst do?
What man will heed the chat of Polish girl,
When the Tsarevitch gives the lie? And learn,
Nor king, nor pope, nor nobles care to know

If these my claims be true, and if I be
Dmitry or some other, it is the same.
I serve as cause for their vile broils and wars,
And that is all they ask. And as for thee,
They soon will find an easy way to still
A rebel's tongue. Farewell!

MARINA.

Tsarevitch, stay!
At last, I hear from thee no boy's lament,
But manly words that bind me to thy lot.
I will forget the story of thy birth:
Before me stands once more Dmitry! But hark,
The hour has struck! Awake! Delay no more!
To Moscow quickly march thy marshalled troops,
The Kremlin clear of foes, the throne possess:
And, if thou wilt, then send to sue my hand.
For God my witness be, till thou hast made
Thy foes a mounting-ladder to the throne,
And till proud Godounoff be driven forth,
No words of love will I consent to hear.

(Exit Marina.)

THE PRETENDER.

No! It is hard to fight with Godounoff,
Or 'gainst the Jesuits at court to plot,
But women harder still! No skill avails.
They coil around, creep slily in and out,
And, hissing, stinging, crawl from out your grasp,
Like slimy serpents! Not in vain I feared
Lest I should fall into her poisoned clutch.
But 'tis resolved! To-morrow morn we march.

SCENE THE SIXTEENTH.

(October 16, 1604.)

The Lithuanian Frontier.

THE PRETENDER. PRINCE KOURBSKY. *Both on horseback, at the head of their troops.*

KOURBSKY. *(Galloping in front).*
Behold, behold! The Russian border-bounds!
My holy fatherland, all hail to thee!
I with disdain shake from my dress the dust
Of stranger earth, and breathe anew with joy
My native air! And now, oh father mine,
Thy soul may rest in peace, thy bones disgraced
Rejoice once more within their prison-grave.
Again the proudest of our heirlooms rich
Shines forth, our sword that filled Kazan with fear,
Our sword, the servant true of Moscow Tsars;
And blood for wine it now shall thirsting drink,
In glory of its hope and liege, the Tsar.

THE PRETENDER.

(Approaching slowly, with bent head.)
How blest is he! With noble pride his soul
Exultant glows and lordly beats with joy!

O knight of purest fame, I envy thee!
Thou son of Kourbsky, reared in exile sad,
Forgetful of the wrongs by sire endured,
His buried fault redeeming at full price,
With eager zeal thy knightly blood wilt shed
For Ivan's son, thy true and lawful Tsar,
Thy bleeding country heal.... Yea, thou art right:
With gladsome pulse thy soul should beat!

KOURBSKY.

And can it be, thy soul beats dull and cold?
It is our Russia calls thee: she is thine.
Across that narrow line her sons await,
Thy Moscow fair, thy Kremlin, and thy throne!

THE PRETENDER.

Alas, the blood of Russia's sons must flow!
Your swords are justly drawn to shield the Tsar;
But I must you against your brethren lead,
Must Litva call to spoil our country dear,
The road to Moscow show her ancient foes!
But let my heavy sin not fall on me;
Boris, Tsar-butcherer, the sin is thine!
Forward!

KOURBSKY.

Forward! March! Woe to Godounoff!
(They ride onwards, whilst the troops cross the frontier.)

SCENE THE SEVENTEENTH.

The Imperial Council Chamber.

THE TSAR. THE PATRIARCH. BASMANOFF. SHOUISKY. BOYARDS.

THE TSAR.

And dare a monk unfrocked, a runaway,
Against us lead his lawless troops, and write
To us his threat'ning letters insolent?
'Tis time this mad adventurer we crushed.
Thou, Troubetskoy, and thou, Basmanoff, see,
My faithful Voyevodes are helped at once:
Relieve the towns and citizens that now
By rebel forces are besieged.

BASMANOFF.

My liege,
Give but three months, and men, I swear by God,
Shall have forgot the name of this base rogue.
Like some show-beast, in foreign country caught,
In iron cage to Moscow will we bring him;
And this I swear!

(Exeunt Basmanoff and Troubetskoy.)

THE TSAR.

     The Swedish King has late
Proposed alliance close and friendship fast;
But we stand not in need of foreign aid;
His offer I refused. Stchelkaloff, send
Command supreme to all our Voyevodes,
That they the number full of horse and men
Enlist, that each religious house supply
Its quota due. In former times, the monks
Themselves, when danger gloomed the common weal,
Were made to serve, and fought on battle-field,
But we would not disturb their holy life,
And bid them keep their cells and pray for us:
Such is the will of Tsar and his Boyards.
And now remains one point we must decide:
You know, the saucy rogue has far and wide
His wild and lying story shameless spread,
By speech and letter, cunningly conceived;
On ev'ry side distrust and fear has sown;
In our squares we hear strange murmurs of revolt;
The minds of men are stirred, they must be calmed.
I would the hour of punishment severe
Forestall, but how? We must at once decide.
I pray thee, father, first thy counsel give.

PATRIARCH.

 Blest be the King of Kings, that He hath sown
Within thy soul, oh dread and mighty Tsar,
Sweet mercy's seed, God's best and chiefest gift!
Nor sinner's death deserved wouldst thou decree,
But, rather, wait till he his error sees;
For it will pass, and righteous truth shine forth,

And lighten all. Thy faithful priest and monk,
Though knowing naught of earthly things and use,
With help of God, presumes to give advice.
This son of evil born, and pervert curst,
Has won, in Dmitry's guise, the people's love;
Like thief in stolen cope, he wears the name
And rank august of the Tsarevitch dead.
That robe we tear from off him, and himself
Shall be revealed in all his naked shame.
And God has sent the means we should employ:
For know, great Tsar, what happed six years ago,
In that same year when thou wert called by God
To rule and guide our orphaned, bleeding land.
In evening hour there came by chance to me
A shepherd plain, in years most reverend,
Who told this story of a marvel strange.

„Whilst yet a child, with blindness I was struck,"
He said, „and from that hour till ripe age,
Nor day nor night I knew; in vain I sought
The aid of herbs, or charms of secret power;
In vain I made my vows, and lowly prayed
Before the shrines of wonder-working saints;
In vain I bathed at sacred wells and streams
My darkened eyes with waters that give life:
The Lord withheld His healing hand of grace.
And in the end I lost all hope, nay, grew
Accustomed to the mist that hemmed me round.
And mystic shapes now ceased to haunt my dreams.
Though oft I heard strange sounds. And once, in sleep
Profound, I heard a childish voice that cried:
Arise, old man, to Uglitch make thy way,

And in cathedral-church, before my tomb,
Repeat thy vows, for God is merciful,
And I will add my helping prayers to thine.
But who art thou? I asked the childish voice.
I am Tsarevitch Dmitry, whom in love
The Lord hath called to join His Angel choir,
And now I am a wonder-working saint:
Go, friend, be healed! And when I woke, methought,
May be, His gift deferred of love He sends;
I go! And straight the distant way I made,
To Uglitch came, and in cathedral-church
Heard mass. My soul unearthly joy did stir,
And tears I shed of sweetness such, it seemed
As if my blindness fell away with them.
And when the church was emptied quite, I said:
Grandson Ivan, conduct me to the grave
Of the Tsarevitch Dmitry. And the boy
Me thither led, and ere my murmured prayer
Was finished half, mine eyes were filled with light:
I saw God's world, my grandson, and the tomb."

Such, Tsar, the marvel strange the old man told.
(All have listened in a state of confused wonder: From time to time Boris wipes away the tears that rise to his eyes.)
I sent some trusty monks to Uglitch straight,
And learned that crowds of sufferers and sick
Have found relief and been to health restored
Before the tomb of young Dmitry murdered.
Now, my advice. Transfer to Kremlin quick,
The sacred relics lay in solemn state;
And thus the people will be brought to see

The patent falsehood of the godless rogue,
And Prince of Evil scattered into dust.
>   *(All are silent for a while.)*

SHOUISKY.

What man can know the secret thoughts of God?
Not ours to sound the depth of mind divine!
Safe from decay the corpse of saintly youth
He can preserve and power unearthly grant;
But none the less with care and patient zeal
Should we pursue the common rumours vague:
Nor find it fit in times of discontent
And riotous revolt to lose our heads
In puzzling out these mysteries profound.
Will men not say, we holy things convert
To tools wherewith to gain a worldly end?
By false reports the people now are stirred,
Made eager to accept each novel tale;
It is not wise to feed the hungry flame
With wonders fresh and marvels yet more strange.
I grant, we must expose the baseless claim,
Uproot the lies, of this bold monk unfrocked:
But we have simpler, surer means at hand.
And if, great Tsar, thou wilt permission give,
I will myself before the people come,
Will speak to them, show how they have been duped,
Convince them of this vain and idle cheat.

THE TSAR.

Let it be so. And, holy father mine,
Forthwith we will withdraw to my own rooms;
I would in private speak with thee to-day.
>   *(Exit, followed by the Boyards.)*

FIRST BOYARD.

(Speaking low to another.)
Didst thou remark, good friend, the Tsar grew pale,
Whilst drops of thickest sweat stood on his face?

SECOND BOYARD.

I do confess, I durst not raise my eyes,
Scarce dared to breathe, much more, to move or stir.

FIRST BOYARD.

'Tis Shouisky alone that rescued us.

SCENE THE EIGHTEENTH.

A Plain near Novgorod-Sieversky.

(December 21. 1604.)

The Field of Battle.

THE PRETENDER. MARGERET. ROSEN. RUSSIAN, GERMAN, AND POLISH SOLDIERS.

SOLDIERS. *(Flying in disorder.)*

Woe to us! Woe to us, Tsarevitch? The Poles! They are on us! We are lost!

(Margeret, Rosen, and others hurry up).

MARGERET.

Whither are you scampering? Allons, back with you, rogues!

ONE OF THE SOLDIERS.

Go back yourself, and if you will, you cursed infidel!

MARGERET.

Quoi? quoi?

ANOTHER OF THE SOLDIERS.

Kwa, kwa! You foreign frog, you dare kwa and croak against the Russian Tsarevitch! You forget, we are pravoslavnie.

MARGERET.

Qu'est-ce à dire, pravoslavnie? Sacrés gueux, maudite canaille! Mordieu, mein Herr, j'enrage: on dirait que ça n'a pas de bras pour frapper, ça n'a que des jambes pour fuir.

ROSEN.

Es ist Schande.

MARGERET.

Ventre-saint-gris! Je ne bouge plus d'un pas; puisque le vin est tiré, il faut le boire. Qu'en dites vous, mein Herr?

ROSEN.

Sie haben Recht.

MARGERET.

Diable, il y fait chaud. Ce diable de Samozvanetz, comme il s'appelle est un brave à trois poils.

ROSEN.

Ja.

MARGERET.

Hé, voyez donc, voyez donc! L'action s'engage sur les derrières de l'ennemi. Ce doit être le brave Basmanoff, qui aurait fait une sortie.

ROSEN.

Ich glaube das.   (*Enter German soldiers.*)

MARGERET.

Ha, ha! voici mes Allemands! Messieurs! Mein Herr, dites leur donc de se rallier, et sacre-bleu, chargeons!

ROSEN.

Sehr gut. Halt!   (*Soldiers draw up in line.*)
Marsch!   (*Soldiers go forward.*)
Hilf Gott! (*General attack: Russian soldiers fly.*)

POLISH SOLDIERS.

Victory! Victory! Hail to Tsar Dmitry!

THE PRETENDER. (*On horseback.*)

Sound the retreat! Victory is ours! Let no more Russian blood be shed! Retreat!
         (*Trumpets sound and drums beat.*)

SCENE THE NINETEENTH.

Square before the Cathedral in Moscow.

A CROWD OF PEOPLE.

FIRST CITIZEN.

Will the Tsar soon come out from the cathedral?

SECOND CITIZEN.

The Liturgy is finished, and they are now chanting the Moleben.

FIRST CITIZEN.

And is it true, they read the Anathema?

THIRD CITIZEN.

I was standing in the porch, and I heard the Reader cry out: „Let Grigory Otrepieff be accursed for ever!"

FIRST CITIZEN.

If they must be cursing, it were better if they cursed themselves! The Tsarevitch has nothing to do with the Otrepieffs.

THIRD CITIZEN.

As to the Tsarevitch, they prayed for the repose of his soul.

FIRST CITIZEN.

Prayed for the repose of the soul of a living man What blasphemy will they next be up to?

THIRD CITIZEN.

Hush! What noise is that? Is it the Tsar?

SECOND CITIZEN.

No, it is the begging-saint.

BOYS.

The brazen night-cap! There goes brazen night-cap!

OLD WOMAN.

Let him alone, you imps of evil! Pray for me, a sinner, holy saint!

BEGGING-SAINT.

Give then, give, give a copeck!

OLD WOMAN.

Here is a copeck. Remember me in thy prayers!

BEGGING-SAINT.

(*Sits on ground and sings.*)
In sky the pale moon creeps,
On earth the kitten weeps;
Arise, thou holy saint,
To God confide thy plaint.

ONE OF THE BOYS.

Good morrow, begging-saint! Why dost thou not take off thy cap? (*Giving a heavy blow on the top of the cap.*) Ah, how hollow it sounds!

BEGGING-SAINT.

I have a whole copeck!

THE BOYS.

It is not true. Show it!
(*They snatch the money out of his hand and run off.*)

BEGGING-SAINT.

They have taken my copeck! They have robbed the poor beggar-saint!

THE PEOPLE.

The Tsar! The Tsar!
(*The Tsar comes out of the cathedral, preceded by Boyards, who scatter money among the crowd.*)

BEGGING-SAINT.

Boris! Boris! The boys have robbed the begging-saint!

THE TSAR.

Give him alms! Why does he weep?

BEGGING-SAINT.

The boys have robbed and insulted me! Bid thy men cut their throats, as thou didst cut the throat of the Tsarevitch.

BOYARDS.

Away, fool! Seize the crazy fool!

THE TSAR.

Let him in peace! Pray for me, holy man!
(*Exit Boris.*)

BEGGING-SAINT. (*Running after him.*)

Nay, nay! I must not pray for the Tsar-Herod! Our Lady will be angry, if I pray for him.

SCENE THE TWENTIETH.

Sievesk.

THE PRETENDER. POLISH SOLDIERS. A RUSSIAN PRISONER.

THE PRETENDER.

Where is the prisoner?

POLISH SOLDIER.

Here.

THE PRETENDER.

Bid him come.
(*Enters Russian prisoner guarded.*)
Thy name?

PRISONER.

Roznoff, a Moscow nobleman.

THE PRETENDER.

How long mayst thou have served?

PRISONER.

Well nigh a month.

THE PRETENDER.

And art thou not ashamed, Roznoff, thy sword 'Gainst me to raise?

PRISONER.

'Tis fate, and not our will.

THE PRETENDER.

At Sieversky thou foughtst?

PRISONER.

I thither came
Two weeks before the battle from Moscow.

THE PRETENDER.

And Godounoff?

PRISONER.

He was alarmed and grieved
At loss of battle, and sent Shouisky
To take command of all the troops.

THE PRETENDER.

But why
To Moscow has Basmanoff been recalled?

PRISONER.

The Tsar his services has well repaid
With rank and gold, and made him Counsellor
At court.

THE PRETENDER.

His place is on the battle-field.
But how fares it at Moscow?

PRISONER.

All goes well.

THE PRETENDER.

My people long to see their Tsar?

PRISONER.

'Tis hard
To tell; of thee wise men have ceased to speak,
Nor care to have their tongue cut out, or lose
Their head. The saying old has come too true:
Each day its sorrow has. The prisons are
Chockful; and if, by chance, two men do meet
In public square.... take heed! some spy is near.
The Tsar himself his leisure time devotes
To hear and probe the rumours of the town.
Once caught, men learn 'tis well to hold their peace.

THE PRETENDER.

Boris his friends an envious life provides!
But pray, how are the troops disposed?

PRISONER.

Of what
Should they complain? They are well-clad, well-fed:
Of course, they are content.

THE PRETENDER.

And what their force?

PRISONER.

None knows.

THE PRETENDER.

Do they to thirty thousand mount?

PRISONER.

Say, rather, fifty thousand, if not more.
(*The Pretender is silent awhile, and the others exchange looks of uneasiness and surprise.*)

THE PRETENDER.

'Tis well. And what report make men of me?

PRISONER.

With us thy mercy all most highly praise,
And grant that, if... forgive the word... a thief,
Thou art most brave.

THE PRETENDER. (*Laughing.*)

And so, in truth, I'll prove
To them. My friends, we will no longer wait
Their Shouisky. Accept my greetings glad:
To morrow we will fight.
(*Exit the Pretender.*)

THE SOLDIERS.

All hail, Dmitry!

FIRST POLISH SOLDIER.

To-morrow we shall fifty thousand fight,
Who number all but fifteen thousand men;
He has gone mad!

SECOND POLISH SOLDIER.

'Tis nothing, friend! One Pole
Five hundred Moscovites may challenge safe.

PRISONER.

Challenge, may be! but when it comes to fight;
Why, from this one the bragging Pole will run.

SECOND POLISH SOLDIER.

And if thou hadst a sword, most saucy rogue,
I would with this for ever close thy mouth.
(Pointing to his sword.)

PRISONER.

We Russians can get on without a sword:
Wouldst like a taste of this, thou brainless Pole?
(Showing his fist.)
*(The Pole looks proudly at him, and goes out silently.
All the others laugh.)*

SCENE THE TWENTY FIRST.

A Forest.

(In the distance a steed is lying on the ground, gasping.)

THE PRETENDER. POUSHKIN. A POLISH SOLDIER.

THE PRETENDER.

My bonnie steed! With what keen joy, this morn,
He proudly galloped forth to his last fight,
And, wounded, bore me from the field unscathed.
My bonnie steed.

POUSHKIN. *(Aside.)*

His horse he weeps and grieves,
Whilst on the plain our troops lie huddled close,
And gnaw the dust.

THE PRETENDER.

But listen, friend, may be,
His wound makes him to lie thus stiff, till he
His strength regains.

POUSHKIN.

He is at his last gasp.

THE PRETENDER.

My bonnie steed! What shall we do? Unloose
The curb, and slack the girth, that at his ease
He may breathe out his life.
(Enter Polish Soldiers.)
Good morrow, sirs.
How comes it that I see not Kourbsky here?
I saw how he through deadly ranks his way
Did hew; a thousand swords flashed round the youth,
As thick as ears of corn, but raising high
His sword above the tallest of his foes,
His bold war-cry was heard above the battle's din.
Where is my knight?

A POLISH SOLDIER.

Stretched on the field of death.

THE PRETENDER.

God grant the hero's soul eternal peace!
How few, alas, have 'scaped the fierce attack!
Those coward loons, the Cossacks of the Don,
May they be damned, betrayed and ruined us,
Nor could three minutes hold and keep their ground.
Let them take heed, for each tenth man I'll hang,
The traitors base!

POUSHKIN.

Whoe'er may be in fault,
One thing we know, we have been crushed, our troops
Mown down, like grass.

THE PRETENDER.

        And all was in our hands!
Within an ace I had their first line trapped,
But quick those Germans sharply cut us off;
In truth, they are real fighters to the core,
I pardon them, that they manœuvred us.
I'll make of them straightway my body-guard.

POUSHKIN.

But where, meanwhile, seek refuge for the night?

THE PRETENDER.

Why, here within the forest we will lodge,
And with the dawn we march, and dine at Rielsk.
Good night! Sweet dreams attend you!
(The Pretender lies down, puts his saddle under his head, and quickly falls asleep.)

POUSHKIN.

          Sweet dreams!
Though all is lost, and we scarce saved our skins,
He throws off care, and sleeps like heedless babe:
Of course, just Providence will guard his days!...
And so, my friends, we will not yet despair.

SCENE THE TWENTY SECOND.

Imperial Apartments in the Kremlin.

THE TSAR. THE TSAREVITCH. BASMANOFF. BOYARDS.

THE TSAR.

We but a fruitless victory have gained;
In vain we crown our brow with laurel wreath.
Anew he has his scattered forces massed,
And from the walls of old Poutlieva threats.
But where are our all-gallant heroes brave?
They stand at Krom, and there a handful small
Of Cossack troops, behind a battered wall,
Hold them at bay. Great cause have we to boast!
On thee I now confer supreme command.
The leader true needs mind, not birth or rank:
Henceforth I'll let them vaunt their rights and claims,
And value at its worth the titled mob,
And give command where merit most deserves.

BASMANOFF.

Ah, Sire, we shall a hundredfold that day
Count blessed, when, with its jealous wranglings low,
And worship of high birth, the Book of Ranks
Be burned in flames.

THE TSAR.

              Nor distant is that day;
I ask but time to quell our rebel folk
And calm their minds.

BASMANOFF.

              That need no trouble cause.
The people to rebel are e'er inclined:
As mettled steed will angry chafe his bit,
So sturdy stripling frets at sire's stern rule:
But what of that? The horseman tames his steed,
And father curbs his son's rebellious will.

THE TSAR.

    And yet, at times, the steed his rider throws;
The son, grown up, casts off the father's rule.
He must be stern and watchful who would bow
The people's heady will. So judged Johann,
The storm-subduer, wisest guide of men;
So judged Ivan the Great, his grandson dread.
Be merciful? As well cast pearls to swine!
Consult their good? They grunt and take the boon;
Oppress? and thy reward is still the same!
What is the news?   (*Enter several Boyards.*)

A BOYARD.

           Some stranger guests are come.

THE TSAR.

  I go, to greet them straight. Basmanoff, stay!
With thee anon I would yet further speak.
                              (*Exit the Tsar.*)

BASMANOFF.

Boris, thou art in soul and mind a Tsar!
God graut thee strength with this Otrepieff curst
To finish once and all! Beneath thy sway,
Shall Russia reap both rich and lasting good.
Thou hast conceived the greatest of reforms,
Nor must we let thy plan grow cold. For me,
A future bright with hopes lies open wide,
If thou but breakst the nobles pompous pride.
No rival on the battle-field I know,
And nearest to the Royal Throne I stand...
Who knows?... What mean those cries and uproar wild?

(General confusion in the rooms of the palace: boyards and attendants running in every direction.)

FIRST BOYARD.

The doctor fetch!

SECOND BOYARD.

The Patriarch call here!

THIRD BOYARD.

Go, summon the Tsarevitch, quick!

FOURTH BOYARD.

For the Confessor send!

BASMANOFF.

What means this noise?

FIFTH AND SIXTH BOYARDS.

The Tsar has swooned, is near to death!

BASMANOFF.

                                              Great God!

FIFTH BOYARD.

  Upon his throne he sat, and sudden fell,
The blood fast flowing from his mouth and ears.
(The Tsar is brought in and placed on a chair. The imperial family and boyards stand around in silence.).

THE TSAR

  Let all withdraw. With the Tsarevitch leave
                    (Exeunt all save Theodore.)
Me here alone... I die... A kiss, and ere I pass...
Farewell, my son, the tawdry crown will soon
Be thine. O God! O God! With all my sins
Unreckoned, unatoned, I come to Thee!
But thou, my son, I feel, art dearer far
Than soul's salvation... so, God's will be done!
A subject born, a subject it behoved to die;
But I to highest point have climbed... Ask not,
By what bye paths! Thou guiltless art;
And thou shalt reign by heritage divine,
And I alone need give account to God.
Oh, dearest son, heed not the honied tongue,
Nor blind thyself and virtues count thy faults.
In stormy times wilt thou be called to rule;
This vain Pretender is no easy foe,
For he with name of dread import is armed.
I, who from youth am trained to power wield,
Have kept in check wild riot and revolt;
Before me men were wont to quake and fear,
Nor dared their treason-thoughts pronounce aloud.

But thou art young, unused to govern men,
How wilt thou, then, when storms rage fierce,
Suppress revolt, the schemes of traitor thwart?
But God is great! and guileless youth makes wise,
The weak endows with strength... Now, listen well:
Without delay, adviser choose, whom thou
Canst trust, in judgment calm and ripe in years,
Loved by the people, a Boyard of rank,
Of noble race, and famous for his deeds:
Say, Shouisky. The troops a leader need
In war well trained and brave: Basmanoff choose,
And firmly brunt the murmuring Boyards.
Whilst young, thou didst with me in Council sit,
And knowest well the order of affairs:
Change not that order, since long custom is
The soul of government. I was compelled
Renew the punishments of death and ban;
Thou canst abolish them, for which thou wilt
Be blessed, as was thine uncle, when the crown
Of dread Ivan the Terrible he wore.
In time and by degrees thou mayst the reins
Of power thou hast relaxed more tightly draw,
But so, that they not once escape thy hands.
All guests from foreign lands with favour greet,
Their services accept with grateful trust.
Above all things the Church protect and watch.
Be niggard of thy speech; the kingly voice
Must not blab empty sounds in vacant air,
But, like cathedral bell, announce alone
The nation's woe, or some event of joy.
Oh, dearest son, thou now hast reached the years,
When woman's charms inflame the heated blood:

Preserve, preserve thy purity of youth,
Taint not thine innocence or pride of shame.
He who in early years becomes the slave
Of passions low and vile, and vicious lust,
Will, when grown up, be sullen and morose,
His mind a prey to doubt and dull distrust.
Be master in thy home, and firmly rule;
Revere thy mother, but thy place maintain
As Tsar and husband both; thy sister love,
Alone remainst to guard her free from ill.

    THEODORE. *(Falling on his knees.)*

 Nay, live! nay live! and reign yet many years!
Without thy saving hand, we all are lost.

    THE TSAR.

  The end is come... 'tis dark... mine eyes grow dim...
I feel the clammy cold of death...
(Enter the Patriarch, Bishops, Boyards, the Tsaritza, who is led into the room, and the Tsarevna, sobbing.)
        Who's there?
The schema?... So, the monkish robe I now
Must wear, the Tsar a peaceful monk become;
My gloomy grave shall be a convent cell.
But, Patriarch, I pray, a moment wait.
I still am Tsar. Receive my last command,
Boyards! Know, this is he on whom my rights
I do confer. The cross I bid you kiss.
Basmanoff, Friends, I, dying, pray you all
In faith and truthfulness to serve him well.
He is so young, as yet unspoiled and pure.
You swear?

BOYARDS.

We swear.

THE TSAR.

I am content.
Forgive the wrongs and ills I may have done,
All acts of petulance, or deeds of private spite...
My father dear, draw nigh. Well, 'tis very well!

SCENE THE TWENTY-THIRD.

A Tent.

BASMANOFF. POUSHKIN.

BASMANOFF.

I pray thee, enter here. and freely speak.
And so, thou hast been sent by him direct?

POUSHKIN.

His friendship true he would to thee propose;
As Moscow Tsar will give thee highest rank.

BASMANOFF.

This same high rank has Theodore conferred,
His army and his troops I now command;
In choosing me he set at naught their claims,
And angered the Boyards.... My oath binds me.

POUSHKIN.

But thou didst swear to serve the lawful heir;
Thy oath is void, if, chance, another lives,
Who has still greater rights.

BASMANOFF.

       Cease, Poushkin, cease!
Wherefore repeat this fable stale? I know
Both who and whence he is.

POUSHKIN.

        And yet, Litva
And Russia long have recognised in him
The true Dmitry. But this I would not urge.
Be he the true Tsarevitch, or a mere
Pretender false, one thing I know and say:
The day must come, it may be soon or late,
This Theodore surrenders him Moscow.

BASMANOFF.

As long as I do serve our youthful Tsar,
So long shall none dare oust him from his throne;
Of troops we have enough, and more, thank God!
Each battle fought shall give them courage fresh;
And tell me, whom will you against me send,
The Cossack, Karela, or Pole, Mniszeck?
And what your force? Eight thousand at the most.

POUSHKIN.

Thou dost mistake: our strength is not in them.
I own myself, our troops are nothing worth;
The Cossacks fit for naught save plunder towns,
For naught the Poles are fit, save boast and drink,
The Russians... but why stay and speak of them?
With thee I will not play the hypocrite.
But wouldst thou know wherein we find our strength?

Not in our troops untrained, nor Polish aid,
But in the people's voice, their firm belief.
Dost thou forget Dmitry's triumphs easy,
And conquests won by magic of his name,
When strongest towns, without a shot or blow,
Have oped their gates, and our raw troops have turned
To flight or captive ta'en thy Voyevodes.
Thyself be judge: have once thy troops shown zeal
To fight with us? Say, when? Whilst Boris lived!
And now?... Nay, friend, the hour is past, to fan
Once more to flame the fire so long extinct:
Thou art with all thy skill and daring doomed
To fail: why court defeat, uphold a cause
Already lost? Show others how to act,
As rightful Tsar thyself proclaim Dmitry,
And win his lasting grace and favour kind.
What dost thou think?

BASMANOFF.

To-morrow shalt thou hear.

POUSHKIN.

Decide.

BASMANOFF.

Farewell!

POUSHKIN.

Consider well my words.
(Exit Poushkin.)

BASMANOFF.

'Tis true! 'Tis true! Dark treason reigns abroad.
What best to do? Shall I thus tamely wait,
Till rebels capture and betray my life,
Into Otrepieff's hands? It wiser were,
Find refuge safe, ere whelming storm hath burst.
But how stands it, if I my sacred oath·
Shall break, and leave my issue name disgraced?
If I the trust and faith of guileless Tsar
With black and foul ingratitude repay?..
The treason-sin of exiled wretch, who smarts
Beneath his cruel wrong, we may forgive;
Not so with me, the trusted, dearly loved,
But death... or power... a people lost... or saved!
Come hither! Who waits there? My steed prepare!

SCENE THE TWENTY FOURTH.

The Place of Execution.

POUSHKIN. A CROWD OF THE PEOPLE.

A VOICE FROM THE CROWD.

By one of the Boyards has the Tsarevitch sent
A message to his people; let us closer stand,
That we may hear.

POUSHKIN.

(Speaking from the Tribune.)
Good Moscow citizens!
His royal greeting the Tsarevitch sends.
(Bows to the People.)
You all do know, how from assassin hands,
Of God's free mercy, was young Dmitry saved;
How God, the top of judgment, had Boris
Struck low, ere he the evil doer reached.
To Dmitry's rule our country now submits:
With lowered arms and loyal humbleness,
Basmanoff sends his troops the oath to take.
To you Dmitry comes with love and peace,
And say, will you, the Godounoff to please,

Lay, impious hands upon the lawful Tsar,
Or rise against great Monomach's grandson?

THE PEOPLE.

Nay, God forbid!

POUSHKIN.

    Good Moscow citizens!
The world doth know the wrongs you have endured
Beneath the haughty upstart's cruel sway;
Extortion, exile, prison, and the block;
Hard toil and hunger,... such your daily lot.
To all alike will Dmitry pity show:
Boyards, the nobles, tradesmen, or allies,
Or clerks,... all honest folk without except.
Will you be obstinate, and, blind, refuse
The proffered boon of mercy unrestrained?
Nor yet forget, the royal throne he mounts
With all the rights of his ancèstors dread.
Fear God and reverence the Tsar, nor dare
Provoke his righteous wrath, but kiss
The cross in homage to his mighty rule;
And send, in sign of peace, without delay
Your bishops, priests, boyards, and delegates,
That lowly they salute their sov'reign Tsar.
    (He descends from the Tribune.)

THE PEOPLE.

No need for idle talk! He speaks the truth.
All hail, Dmitry! All hail, the Tsar Dmitry!

A PEASANT.

(Mounting the Tribune.)
To Kremlin Palace let us go, good friends,
And seize the squeaking cubs of Godounoff!

THE PEOPLE.

(Rushing forward in Crowds.)
We'll seize and strangle them! All hail, Dmitry!
And cursèd be Boris and his whole race!

SCENE THE TWENTY FIFTH.

The Kremlin. House of the Godounoffs. Sentinel before the Door.

THEODORE. KSENIA SENTINEL. BEGGAR. CROWD OF THE PEOPLE.

BEGGAR.

(To Theodore who is standing at the window.)
For Christ's sake, give a trifle to the poor!

SENTINEL.

Move on; it is forbidden to speak with the prisoners.

THEODORE.

Come here, old man. I am the poorer of us two! Thou, at least, art free.
(Ksenia, closely veiled, also comes near to the window.)

FIRST CITIZEN.

Look, the brother and sister, poor things, like birds in cage confined.

SECOND CITIZEN.

Why throw away pity on them? Accursed race!

FIRST CITIZEN.

The father, it is true, was guilty; but these poor children have done no wrong.

SECOND CITIZEN.

Rubbish! they are chips of the old block.

KSENIA.

Brother, brother! It seems, those Boyards there are coming to us.

THEODORE.

That is Golitzine, and that Mosalsky. The others I know not.

KSENIA.

Ah, darling, my heart misgives me.
(Golitzine and three Boyards come on to the square, followed by three Archers.)

THE PEOPLE.

Make room there! Room for the Boyards!
(The Boyards enter the House of the Godounoffs.)

FIRST CITIZEN.

What have they to do there?

SECOND CITIZEN.

Most likely to make Theodore Godounoff take the oath.

FIRST CITIZEN.

Thinkest so? But listen, what is that noise in the house?
All is hurry and confusion!

SECOND CITIZEN.

Dost thou hear that shriek? A woman's voice! Let us go in!
The doors are closed. The cries are hushed, but the noise continues.
(The doors are thrown open, and Mosalsky appears on the threshold.)

MOSALSKY.

Citizens! Marie Godounoff and her son, Theodore, have poisoned themselves. We have seen their dead bodies. (*The people are silent with horror.*) Why remain you silent? Cry out with me: Long live the Tsar, Dmitry Ivanovitch!

(The people continue silent.)

EXPLANATORY NOTES.

EXPLANATORY NOTES.

Page 3. *The Dreamer.* In 1818, Poushkin, having quitted the Lyceum, became member of the once famous Arzamas Club, which was founded in 1815, with the design of defending the new style and principles of literature adopted by Karamsin. Each member, on being elected, was required, by way of introduction, to present an original composition in verse, and Poushkin selected for this purpose the eighth and ninth stanzas of a poem, entitled *The Dreamer,* written three years earlier, and first published in the October number of the *Russian Museum,* a journal in which many of the poet's youthful compositions originally appeared.

Page 6. *The Grave of a Youth.* These lines, though not published till 1826, were written in the autumn of 1821, as a tribute of affection to the memory of Korsakoff, a young Lycean, who died very suddenly, whilst on a visit with his parents to Florence. They are characterised by that tone of reserve and simplicity of thought and language, which give such a rare charm to Poushkin's verse.

Page 8. The lines, *I have Outlived my Every Wish,* were written during the poet's exile to Kischeneff. They are naturally the outcome of a smarting sense of injustice. In their tone they represent most strikingly the Russian character, and express a feeling of quiet, despairing indifference, so unlike the defiant passion that made Byron revolt against the wrongs he was called on to suffer. They were first published in 1823, under the title of *An Elegy*.

Page 8. Poushkin's ode, *To The Sea,* in memory of Napoleon, his favourite hero, and Byron, his favourite poet, was originally published in 1824. Several changes were made in it, when the poet, in 1826, revised it for publication in the first collected edition of his works. The stanza, beginning with the words, „the world is dull and empty", was struck out by the censor, in consequence of the too evident allusion in its last line; and only long after the death of the poet was it allowed to be printed. The ode, it must be remembered, was written soon after Poushkin's departure from the south of Russia for his family estate at Michaelovsky, in the government of Pskoff.

Page 11. There is every reason to believe that Poushkin's *Elegy* is not a fancy-piece, but that it was suggested by the death of a near lady-friend. Numerous attempts have been made to discover her name, but without success. The manuscript of the poem bears the date, July 29, 1826, and has also these words, written in an abbreviated form: „I have just heard of the death of..." In the original copy, the first line runs as follows: „Beneath the deep-blue sky of her native Italy."

Page 11. *Vain Gift, Gift of Chance.* Poushkin had already passed the Sturm und Drang period in his career, when he wrote, in 1828, his touching lines, *Vain Gift, Gift of Chance.* Their perfect melody of verse is in complete harmony with the delicacy of thought they convey, and they but too truly interpret the disenchantment that for a while overcame the poet, and from which he was only saved when he had come to learn that true art is alien to the political turmoil and sordid interests of the day.

Page 12. *Drowned.* This little fantastic legend, told in the homely language of the people is one of the best known and most popular of Poushkin's shorter poemś. It was written in 1828. In the sixth stanza occur two expressions it may be well to explain. In the houses of the peasantry, even to the present day. a kind of lath torch, called *louchiéna*, is stuck into a chink in the wall, and, when lighted, serves as candle, or lamp. The shelf, called *palátie,* is a large, wooden plank, stretching from the top of the stove to the wall of the cottage, and which is used as a bed.

Page 15. *The Unwashed.* Not only by birth, but in heart and feeling, Poushkin was an aristocrat, and never entirely freed himself from that contemptuous pity with which the Russian nobleman is wont to think and speak of the poor peasant. In none of his poems has he expressed this feeling with such unpleasant frankness as in *The Unwashed,* first published in 1829, in one of the Moscow journals. We must regard it as the true artist's stern protest against those who would have the poet be nothing more than a teacher of the world's ordinary morality, by whose observance men can secure its approval and win to themselves reputation and ease. In a later poem, entitled *The Poet,* and written when Poushkin had gained a larger and sadder experience of the responsibilities of life, we shall find a higher and more ideal appreciation of the poet's calling.

Page 17. *A Winter Morning.* These lines were written in 1829, and form one of a series of short descriptive sketches· For simplicity of thought and purity of language, they may be compared with our English Cowper's charming pictures of winter scenery. Writing at a time when the critical authorities of his country expected a poet to observe the rules of classical style and diction, Poushkin dared to employ homely words and to describe familiar scenes of daily life. He thus enlarged the sphere and domain of poetry, and brought it into unison with our commonest and most ordinary experiences.

Page 18. *The Joys of Thoughtless Years are Spent.* Written at Bodlino, in 1834, this Elegy was published the same year in the *Library for Reading,* a Moscow monthly journal.

Page 19. *A Study.* „Let pleasure be my law", is the refrain of one of Poushkin's earlier poems. Of course, the „monotony of life's riot" soon began to pall, and his long enforced exile from the capital revealed to him new scenes that were calculated to arouse within him a deeper sympathy than he had hitherto experienced with the sufferings and deprivations of the poorer classes of his country. They became to him something more than the „unwashed mob"; and in *A Study,* written in 1830, though only published in 1841, we have a sketch, which all who are acquainted with Russian peasant-life will recognise to be true in its every detail.

Page 20. The grand lines addressed to the calumniators of Russia were written in the autumn of 1832, but were not published during the poet's lifetime. It is curious to remark that they were not allowed, in spite of their patriotic tone, to be included in the first edition of Poushkin's collected works. They were mainly called forth by the position taken up towards Russia by the great Polish poet, Mickiewicz. It will be observed that, during the comparatively short interval that had elapsed since the composition of his ode, *To the Sea*, Poushkin had outgrown his youthful worship of Napoleon, whose „brutal rule" is now vigorously denounced.

Page 22. *The Poet.* Like Tennyson, in his poem of the same title, Poushkin, in *The Poet,* written in 1830, exalts the mission of the true singer, who must be a law into himself, and must teach what he knows to be the truth, careless of public praise, and whose sole reward should be the consciousness that his song is the sincere and unalloyed outcome of his soul.

Page 22. *God Grant, My Reason Ne'er Betray Me.* There were times in the life of Poushkin, as in the life of every great poet, when he thought too deeply and brooded too nicely on the puzzle of the world; when, indeed, the strain upon his reason grew so intense, that he feared lest his mind should become unhinged. It was under the influence of such feeling that he wrote the lines, *God Grant My Reason Ne'er Betray Me.* They were written in 1833, the year in which he composed *The Bronze Cavalier,* one of the greatest and most characteristic of his productions. Like Paracelcus, he prays God, the Master-Mind, to whom mind should be dear, to ward off the dreaded curse. Poushkin's artistic temperament is shown in the fear that, with the loss of reason, he may gaze up to the heavens, and find them empty.

Page 24. *My Monument.* „The more Poushkin became a true poet," writes Gogol, „the more closely he interpreted the feelings common to all real poets, the colder grew the reception he met at the hands of the reading-public, and the number of his admirers dwindled away, till he could easily count them on his fingers." Keenly sensitive to criticism, Poushkin felt the injustice meted out to him by the mob, and in more than one poem has expressed his resentment. It is to this same feeling we may attribute the composition of *My Monument,* written in 1836, the year preceding his death, and in which he makes appeal from contemporary prejudice, and boldly predicts immortality to his verse.

Page 27. *The Gipsies,* written in 1824, is, perhaps, the most interesting of Poushkin's earlier poems. In the story of its hero, Aleko, Poushkin teaches the lesson which he himself had to learn in his exile. We cannot, without injury to ourselves, repay the injustices the world may have done us, by a contemptuous defiance of all law. Nor need we think to find happiness in a life of wild freedom, in which we acknowledge no authority save our own will. Man must live for others, and in Aleko's silent acquiescence in the sentence that banished him from the gipsy camp, we may recognise his confession of the justice of his fate. As in nearly all that Poushkin wrote during the first stage of his poetical career, in *The Gipsies* there is a Byronic colouring both in the incidents of the story and in the conception of the heroine's character.

Page 34. *A stranger.* In his story of „the banished stranger," the Old Man alludes to Ovid.

Page 55. Though entitled *Poltava,* the decisive battle fought near that place on July 8. 1709, forms but an episode in the poem, and its hero is, not Peter the Great, but Mazeppa. Indeed, according to the original plan, the poem was to have been called after the Hetman, but Poushkin subsequently changed the title, in order that it might not clash with Byron's poem of the same name. The character of Mazeppa is sketched after the popular tradition, but more recent researches have proved that the aim of all his schemes and plots was to secure the independence of Little Russia. In the poem he is represented as a cold intriguer, to whom love, freedom, fatherland, are empty names, and who, to avenge an affront he had received from the Tsar during a drunken carousal, consents to betray his country. The beauty of the poem resides in the delineation of the old Hetman's love for the young Marie, daughter of Kotzubei. In no preceding or later Russian poet do we find such a keen and subtle study. It is not necessary to direct the reader's attention to the beautiful description of night in the Ukraine, to the grand portrait of Peter on the field of battle, or to the scene between the imprisoned Kotzubei and Orlick. The poem was written within the short period of a month, but, though composed in October 1828, it was not published till late in the autumn of the following year.

Page 56. *His messengers the Hetman sends.* Mazeppa offered his hand in marriage to Matrona, Kotzubei's youngest daughter, but his suit was rejected.

Page 66. *Lord of Fate.* Referring to Napoleon's disastrous retreat from Moscow.

Page 61. Doroschenko, one of the heroes of ancient Little Russia, and the implacable enemy of Russian rule.

Page 61. Grigory Samoilovitch, son of the Hetman, was exiled to Siberia in the first year of the reign of Peter the First.

Page 61. Palaeus, celebrated as a daring horseman, was, through the intrigues of Mazeppa, sent into exile, whence he returned only when the Hetman's treachery had been discovered.

Page 61. Gordienko, a Cossack Ataman, who went over to Charles the Twelfth, but in 1708 was taken prisoner and put to death.

Page 61. Bogdan, the greatest of Little Russian rulers, was leader of the fierce revolt against the tyranny of the Polish nobles, and till his death in 1657 enjoyed the trust and confidence of the people.

Page 65. Iskra, a colonel in one of the Poltava regiments, was Kotzubei's friend and confident.

Page 67. The Jesuit Zalenskoi, the Princess Dulskaya, and a Bulgarian prelate, who had been banished from his country, were the chief agents employed by Mazeppa. The last of these three, disguised as an almsman, was mainly engaged in conveying secret information between Poland and the Ukraine.

Page 67. Orlick, a Government Secretary, after the death of Mazeppa in 1710, received from Charles the Twelfth the title of Hetman of Little Russia. He subsequently adopted the Mahomedan faith, and died at Bender in 1726.

Page 68. Bolavine, a Cossack of the Don, who about this time put himself at the head of a military revolt.

Page 80. *The village of Dianka.* Dianka is the name of one of the villages on the Poltava estate of the Kotzubeis.

Page 82. After Kotzubei had been cast into prison, he was, at the command of the Hetman, subjected to the torture, under the pretext of extorting from him the names of his abettors, but in reality to discover where he had, under fear of arrest, concealed the greater part of his moneys and wealth.

Page 92. *For Swedish slain prepares a place.* We have the same idea expressed in the last couplet of Poushkin's lines, *To the Calumniators of Russia:*

„In Russian plains we'll find them place
To sleep with those who fell before."

Page 92. *Another chief the Cossacks choose.* On November 7. 1708. the Cossacks elected Skoropadsky, one of their colonels, to the place of Hetman.

Page 93. Tchetchel, Ataman of the Zaporovian districts that is, the districts lying beyond the Dnieper Rapids, is chiefly famous for the obstinacy with which he defended Batourine against Menschikoff and his troops.

Page 94. *Sup at Dresden.* Voltaire, in the concluding paragraph of the third Book of *L'Histoire de Charles XII*, has told the story of the Swedish King's madcap visit to Augustus II at Dresden.

Page 94. *With a jest defiance take.* Whilst Charles was dictating a letter to one of his secretaries, a bomb was shot into the tent and fell near the table at which the latter was writing. „Ah, your majesty, a bomb!" he exclaimed, leaping up in fright. „What has a bomb to do with what I am dictating to you? Please, write on: „was the King's rejoinder.

Page 94. *Cossacks sitting round the fire.* One night Charles set out alone to spy the Cossack camp, and came on soldiers that were sitting round a fire. He straightway shot at them with his pistol, whereupon they replied, and one of them wounded the King in the leg.

Page 99. *Unmoved the leaders calmly watched.* As we read these lines, we are reminded of Dick Steele's wise criticism on Addison's *Compaign,* in which a like unnatural calmness on the battlefield is attributed to Marlborough. See Thackeray's *Esmond.* Book II, chapter XI.

Page 101. *Teachers in the art of war.* „Alors prenant un verre de vin," writes Voltaire, „à la santé, dit l'empereur, de mes maitres dans l'art de la guerre. Renschild lui demanda : qui étaient ceux qu'il honorait d'un si beau titre ? Vous, messieurs, les généraux Suédois, reprit le Tsar. Votre Majesté est donc bien ingrate, reprit le Comte, d'avoir tant maltraité ses maitres."

Page 109. Written in 1830, Poushkins *Mozart and Saglieri* was first published in 1832. There is no historical basis for the sketch beyond the fact that, at the first representation of *Don Juan,* a loud sharp hiss from a remote part of the Prague theatre, where it was produced, interrupted the admiring applause with which it was received; and immediately after the famous Saglieri was seen to quit the house, pale with anger and envy. „There is no injustice done to his memory," writes Poushkin, „in supposing that the man who hissed *Don Juan* would be guilty of poisoning its composer."

Page 125. *The Bronze Cavalier,* written in 1833, owing to difficulties raised by the censors, was not published till after the poet's death. It is a story of the terrible inundation in 1824, when the whole of Petersburg was overflowed, and hundreds of lives were lost. It may be regarded as an apotheosis of Russia's glorious hero, and forms a worthy close to Poushkin's literary career. What, perhaps, strikes us most in the original is the rare force, flexibility, and grand simplicity of its verse. „We should like," writes Belinsky, the greatest of Russian critics, „to have said something on this point; but any adequate praise of its verse should be couched in rythmic language as grand and powerful, and it is beyond our weak and halting prose to pronounce its fitting eulogy." Much of this beauty of style must be lost in any translation, though we have done our best to preserve something of the charm and energy of the original.

Page 145. Beyond the names of its leading personages, Poushkin's *Statue Guest* has little in common with Molière's *Don Juan,* or with Da Ponte's *Il Dissoluto Punito.* Poushkin, instead of adapting the old legend, has introduced two important variations, and has thus succeeded in giving his piece a dramatic continuity of intérest. By representing Donna Anna, not as the daughter, but as the widow of the Commander, and by making her first interview with Juan take place, not before, but after her husband's death, the poet compels us to acknowledge the over-ruling power of a mysterious implacable fate, that hurries on events to their predestined end. In this way, the second scene ceases to be, as at first sight we are tempted to regard it, a mere episode, and becomes an essential contingency in the fated career of the hero. When he visits Laura, he meets Don Carlos, the Commander's brother, and in the rash challenge that ensues and causes the death of Carlos, the original curse that lies upon the slayer of Donna Anna's spouse first asserts its power by inspiring Juan with an overweening belief in his success, a false trust in the supremacy of his lucky star. It is this assurance that provokes him to his final act of blasphemous daring, when he invites the Statue to keep watch as sentinel at the door of the widow's room during their loving interview. In the vulgarer version of the legend, the appearance of the Statue is but the romancist's ordinary *Deus ex machinâ;* in Poushkin's drama, it is the fated outcome and necessary consequence of Juan's defiance of the laws of God and men. The *Statue Guest,* written in 1830, was first published in 1839 in a popular collection of Russian poems and novels, issued by Smerdine, a Moscow editor.

Page 187. The publication in 1820 of the tenth volume of Karamsin's *History of Russia*, which is devoted to the years immediately succeeding the death of Ivan the Terrible, suggested to Poushkin the idea of his tragedy, *Boris Godounoff*, and it is to the historian that the drama is dedicated. Strictly speaking, it cannot be called a tragedy, but is rather a series of dramatic scenes, in which the portrait of Godounoff, as drawn by Karamsin, is closely followed. But whatever objections may be urged against the form given to the play, we need only turn to the tragedies of preceding writers, such as Ozereff's *Dmitry of the Don*, to be convinced that Poushkin's *Boris Godounoff* opens a new era in the history of the Russian theatre. It is manifestly written under the influence of Shakspeare, whose works, we know, Poushkin was at that time studying. This is particularly evident in the scenes where the citizens play the principal part, in the scene where the Pretender and his followers cross the Lithuanian frontier, as well as in the highly dramatic interview between Boris and Shouisky, where the former, having scouted Shouisky's information concerning the reappearance of the buried Dmitry as „most mirth-provoking", suddenly turns upon him with the query: „Well, what? Say, why thou dost not laugh?" Although detached portions of the tragedy were published between the years 1827 and 1830, it was only in 1831 that, with the omission of scene the sixth, the work appeared in its full and complete form.

Page 187. Shouisky, a direct descendant of Rurick, after the death of Boris in 1605, put himself at the head of the conspirators against the Pretender, and, having slain the false Dmitry, mounted the throne. During the troubled days that followed the appearance of a second Pretender, known in history as the Tuschino Rogue, Shouisky with great difficulty maintained his power, and in 1610 was completely defeated by the Polish army, and compelled to abdicate and retire to a monastery. Of Vorotinsky nothing is known, beyond that he was one of Shouisky's most devoted followers.

Page 187. *Patrol the streets.* On all public occasions, when the people were likely to gather in large numbers in the streets of Moscow, a certain number of Boyards patrolled the city to preserve order.

Page 188. Tcheptchougoff was secretly engaged by Boris to poison the Tsarevitch Dmitry, but at the last moment refused to carry out the instructions he had received.

Page 189. Michael Bietargovsky was appointed by Godounoff, to be governor of the town of Uglitch. His son Danelo accompanied him, together with his nephew, Katchaloff. All three were intimately concerned in the murder of the young Dmitry.

Page 190. Godounoff was of Tartar origin, and married the daughter of Malouta Skouratoff, who through his cruelty won to himself the surname of hangman.

Page 197. *Fate calls me to succeed the Angel-Tsar.* In character and by nature Theodore was extremely gentle, and amongst the people he was always called the Angel-Tsar.

Page 198. *Our subjects all.* Karamsin tells us that on the day Boris assumed the crown all the people of Moscow, „from the Patriarch to the lowest beggar," were invited to dine with the Tsar in his palace at the Kremlin.

Page 200. In the history of the Pretender we meet with the name of Peamen, a monk who accompanied Otrepieff when he crossed the Lithuanian frontier. But, as Pouchkin himself has told us, in Peamen he has drawn, not the character of any individual monk, but has rather portrayed those qualities which in general distinguished the monks of the sixteenth and seventeenth centuries.

Page 201. It is still an open question who the False Demetrius really was. Kostomaroff frankly acknowledges himself unable to propose any satisfactory solution of the mystery. Poushkin has accepted the popular tradition, according to which he was a runaway monk, who secretly escaped from Moscow in 1602. It is, however, difficult to believe that in the short space of two years 'he could have completely transformed himself into a Polish noble, learned to speak the language fluently, and become an excellent swordsman and rider.

Page 201. *The streets of Novgorod.* Referring to the cruel measures adopted by Ivan to suppress the revolt of Novgorod in 1570. For five days a general massacre of men, women, and children took place, during which thousands were first tortured and then put to death.

Page 203. *Under Shouisky.* That is, Ivan Petrovitch Shouisky, uncle to the Shouisky in Poushkin's tragedy, and of whom mention is made in the first scene.

Page 204. *Sought full peace of soul.* From Karamsin we learn that Ivan was accustomed to vary the monotony of massacring discontented or suspected subjects by making so-called „religious journeys," during which he would visit the more celebrated monasteries of his empire. In a letter written to the Prior of Bielozersky Monastery, he speaks of having met there and conversed with the monks Nicodemus, Serge, and Cyril.

Page 204. Theodore, son of Ivan the Terrible, reigned for nearly fourteen years, but was all the while under the guidance of Godounoff, his wife's brother. By nature he was „very gentle, of an easy disposition, quiet, merciful, and not martially inclined". He died in 1598, and immediately after his death his widow entered a convent and took the veil.

Page 205. *The monstrous crime.* In his description of the murder of Dmitry, Theodore's half-brother, Poushkin has closely followed Karamsin. The three murderers were Michaeloff, Katchaloff, and Volchoff. The crime was committed on May 15, 1591, when, during the temporary absence of the Tsaritza,

and in spite of the brave attempts of his foster-mother to save
the boy, he was betrayed by one of his nurses into the hands
of his assassins. They were all three seized by the people
and put to death, after having confessed that they had acted
according to the instructions given them by Boris.

Page 208. This scene was first published in 1833 in the
January number of the *Dorpater Jahrbuch für Litteratur,
Statistik und Kunst*. At the urgent advice of Mickiewicz, it was
suppressed by Poushkin in the first complete edition of the
tragedy, though subsequently included as a supplementary
scene. It is not difficult to understand why Mickiewicz wished
it to be struck out. Not only is it written in a metre different
to that employed in the rest of the tragedy, but in spirit and
tone it is inconsistent with the character of the Pretender.
Its defects are all the more patent, inasmuch as it immediately
follows the grand scene in Peamen's cell between Grigory
and the chronicler-monk.

Page 211. We read in Karamsin that a young monk of
Tchudoff, named Grigory, once jokingly exclaimed to some
of his companions: „You know, one day I shall be Tsar of
Moscow!" These imprudent words were brought to the ears
of the Metropolitan, who reported to the Patriarch, „that a
certain monk, Grigory, had fallen into a damnable heresy, and
had indulged in unseemly speech." The good-natured Patriarch left the report unnoticed, but the Tsar, having been informed of it, ordered the „madman" to be imprisoned for life
in the Solovetsky Monastery. Happily, the unfortunate monk,
through the services of a certain Eupheme, was enabled to
escape before the sentence could be put into execution. No
attempt was made to arrest him, and his flight was kept a
secret from the Tsar.

Page 214. *A raging fire*. Referring to the terrible fire,
which on the eve of Trinity Sunday, 1591, destroyed the greater
part of the city. Whilst Karamsin leaves the origin of the fire
an open question, the chroniclers are at one in attributing it

to Godounoff, who, by his lavish generosity to those who had lost their all, won over the people to his side, at least for a time.

Page 215. *Her youthful lord laid low.* Prince Johann of Denmark, a few days after his arrival in Moscow, in 1602, to celebrate his betrothal with the Tsarevna Ksenia, sickened of a fever, and died.

Page 219. *A regular St. George's Day for me.* In early times the Russian peasants enjoyed the right of changing their domicile on St. George's Day, that is, towards the end of the agricultural year. Of this right they were deprived by an ukaz issued in 1592 by Boris Godounoff, and serfdom was established in Russia. The expression, Saint George's Day, is therefore equivalent to an unlucky day.

Page 225. The portrait here drawn of Grigory Otrepieff tallies in every respect with the description contemporary writers give of the Pretender.

Page 228. *Athanasius Michaelovitch.* The real name of this Poushkin, an ancestor of the poet, was Eustathius Michaelovitch. He was one of the ambassadors sent in 1595 to conclude a treaty, by which the Swedes' agreed to restore to Russia the Novgorod towns and cities they had taken possession of. Together with his two brothers, he was in 1601 exiled to Siberia, mainly on the testimony of his servants, who pretended he was engaged in a plot against Boris.

Page 228. Gabriel Grigorovitch Poushkin is first mentioned in Karamsin's history as having been sent in 1605 to Krasnoe Selo, near Moscow, to read publicly the Pretender's manifesto, announcing his claim to the throne, and to excite the people against Godounoff's dynasty.

Page 229. *The King's own private room.* The Jesuit after a while succeeded in overcoming Sigismund's hesitancy, and persuaded him to receive the Pretender in audience in the private room of his palace. „The King," we are told, by the Court Secretary, „welcomed Grigory with a smile and with a friendly shake of the hand.

Page 230. *In Visnevetsky's house*. Grigory served in the house of Visnevetsky, and through his modest bearing and skill in martial exercises won general trust and confidence. After he had been there some months, he pretended to fall seriously ill, sent for the family priest, and, having first confessed, said in a low tone: „I am dying. Lay my body in the earth with all the honours due to one of princely rank. When I have closed my eyes in death, take and read the papers you will find concealed under my bed." The priest, who was a Jesuit, at once informed Visnevetsky of what had taken place, and the latter, having found the papers, read, to his astonishment, that the supposed servant was no other than Dmitry. He did all in his power to restore Grigory to health, cunningly spread the news abroad, and the whole of Lithuania resounded with the marvellous story.

Page 230. *His aid has sworn*. Sigismund undertook to furnish Grigory with an annual subsidy of 54,000 roubles.

Page 231. *On the bloody pale*. In the year 1565, Prince Dmitry Schevreiff was impaled by order of Boris. But no sufferings could break the courage of the brave man, and all day long he repeated in a calm and distinct voice prayers and hymns of faith.

Page 231. *With staff the ashes rakes*. This reminds us of Occleve's description, in his *Governail of Princes*, of the burning of Badby, the blacksmith, to whom, when he was brought to the stake, the Prince of Wales spake kindly and urged recantation, but, after Badby had refused to deny his faith, stirred up with his stick the fuel heaped around him, that it might burn the more fiercely.

Page 231. The princes Schietsky, Schistounoff, and Romanoff were all seized in the year 1601, and immured in different monasteries. According to one account, Romanoff, his wife, and two children were confined and starved to death in an underground cell in the Bielozersky Monastery.

Page 233. *As easily as the dew.* In old Russian songs we frequently find this comparison between the dew and the tears of a young bride or wife, as for instance in the following lines, translated by M*r* Ralston in his *Songs of the Russian People:*

„There weeps his mother... as a river runs;
There weeps his sister... as a streamlet flows;
There weeps his youthful wife... as falls the dew;
The sun will rise and gather up the dew."

Page 234. *A map of Muscovy.* Cruel as a ruler, Boris was a kind husband and father. He gave the best possible education to his children. The map of Russia drawn by Theodore has been preserved, and was published in 1614 by the German painter, Gerard.

Page 235. Simon Godounoff was a grand-officer of the crown. Karamsin relates how in 1604 he was sent at the head of some troops to Astrachan against some rebel Cossacks, who, having defeated the royal forces, despatched a company of archers to Moscow with this message: „Tell Boris that before a month is over, we shall enter Moscow with Dmitry, the Tsarevitch."

Page 241. *The crown of Monomach.* In the Arsenal at Moscow are still preserved the „gold cap," or crown of Monomach, together with the chain, imperial globe, sceptre, and epaulets, which were sent by the Byzantine Emperor as a present to Vladimir Monomach, Prince of Kieff. These ornaments are used at the coronation of the Russian Tsars. Vladimir, who died in 1125, is one of the earliest Russian writers and is the author of a curious book, entitled *Instructions,* and treating of the qualities necessary to a good prince.

Page 242. *I warrant.* The Pretender bound himself in writing that he would, in the course of one year after his accession, cause Russia to be united to the Western Church. He also promised that Marina Mniszeck, when Tsaritza, should be allowed to erect catholic monasteries. It was further stipulated that, if he failed to fulfil his promise, „Marina was free to divorce herself from him, unless she had sufficient patience to wait a second year".

Page 244. *I am his son.* André Kourbsky won no little renown at the siege of Kazan. He subsequently fell into disgrace under Ivan, and to escape punishment fled to Volmar, then in possession of the Lithuanian troops, and went over to the Polish party. The latter years of his life were passed in Volhynia, on an estate granted him by the King of Poland, but were greatly embittered by unavailing regret at the part he had played against his country.

Page 244. Olga's city. That is, Pskoff; the city being dedicated to Saint Olga.

Page 245. Chroustchoff was sent by the Tsar on a mission to the Cossacks of the Don. They seized him, and brought him in chains to Grigory. On coming into the presence of the Pretender, Chroustchoff fell on his knees, and cried out: „In thy face I recognise the face of Ivan: I am thy slave, and will serve none other all my life." His services were accepted, and he became one of the warmest supporters of the Pretender.

Page 252. *And, lo, 'tis done.* „The chief and principal adviser, in this march to Moscow," writes Karamsin, „was Mniszeck, who, in spite of his age, was extravagantly ambitious and ridiculously lightminded. He had a young and beautiful daughter, Marina, who was as ambitious and lightminded as her father. The Pretender, during his stay at Mniszeck's castle in Sambore, declared himself her lover, and easily turned her head by giving her in anticipation the title of Tsaritza, and the delighted father eagerly consented to their union in the hope of seeing the whole of Russia at the feet of his daughter."

Page 266. *My faithful Voyevodes.* Most of the early Russian ranks and titles are of a military character. Voyevode is the head of the forces called out in case of war. The word is derived from *voi,* or *boi,* battle, aud *vodiet,* to lead. To the same root, *boi,* is to be traced the word, boyard.

Page 267. *In former times.* In one of Godounoff's proclamations we read: „There have been times when our monks, priests, and almoners took up arms and fought, and freely shed their blood in defence of the country. But we have no wish they should do so now. Let them keep in their monasteries and pray for the welfare of the Tsar. In the reign of the great Ivan, at one and the same time, Russia warred with the Sultan, with Lithuania, with Sweden, and with the Crimean Khans. What, then, can she have to fear from a miserable rebel like this Grigory Otrepieff?"

Page 273. *Pravoslavnie:* that is, members of the orthodox Eastern Church.

Page 273. *Pas de bras.* In this battle, as on other occasions, the Russian troops, persuaded in their hearts that Grigory was the true Tsarevitch, fought faintheartedly and fled at the first rebuff. The reproach here put into the mouth of the Frenchman, Margeret, who, together with the Lithuanian nobleman, Walter Rosen, was the most zealous of Godounoff's allies, is transcribed, word for word, from Karamsin's History.

Page 273. The Russian word, *Samozvanetz,* literally selfnamer, signifies Pretender.

Page 275. The Liturgy, corresponding with the Catholic Mass, is followed on solemn occasions by the Moleben, or prayers for the Tsar, the Imperial Family, persons in authority, and all orthodox Christians.

Page 276. *Brazen Night-cap.* At this time there was a fanatic, who enjoyed great popularity at Moscow for his supposed saintliness. He used to haunt the streets of the city, wearing a huge watercarrier's cap made of brass, was very lightly dressed even in the severest frost, and in a mournful voice would chant prophecies of the woe that should befall the usurping Boris. He was known among the people under the nickname of Brazen Nightcap. Godounoff was afraid to arrest or punish him, so great was the reverence in which he was generally held.

Page 282. *To-morrow we will fight.* In this scene we have an animated picture of the difficulties the Pretender had to encounter in his march to Moscow. His whole force, horse and infantry, did not amount to more than 16,000 men, whilst the Tsar's army consisted of not less than 65,000 men. It was the turning-point in his career. He was driven to give battle to the imperial troops, in order to escape being hemmed in at Sievsk, and cut off from all communication with the towns where his supporters were.

Page 286. *I'll make of them.* On his march to Moscow, the Pretender was accosted by a body of Germans, who offered their services. They were most flatteringly received, and Grigory said to them: „I have greater trust in you, than I ever can have in my Russian troops." He chose three hundred of them to form his bodyguard.

Page 290. *Let all withdraw.* The dying words addressed by Boris to his son, Theodore, remind us of those spoken by Bolingbroke to Harry, Prince of Wales, in Shakspere's *Henry the Fourth*, Part II, Act IV, Scene 4.

Page 291. *Basmanoff choose.* Immediately after the death of Boris Godounoff, which took place on April 13, 1605,

Theodore, then in his sixteenth year, chose Prince Mstieslavsky and the two Princes Vassiely and Dmitry Shouisky to be his chief counsellors, and appointed Basmanoff to be commander-in-chief of the army.

Page 292. *The schema.* The name of the dress worn by monks of the Greek church. There are two different kinds: the great schema, worn by monks of the higher ranks, and the little schema, worn by those of lower grades.

Page 296. *To-morrow shalt thou hear.* It was on May 7 that Basmanoff openly espoused the cause of the Pretender, though he knew, as he himself confesses to Poushkin, who and whence Grigory really was. „The treachery of Basmanoff," writes Karamsin, „was a mystery to his contemporaries; it is equally a mystery to their descendants." We may suppose that, convinced of the army's adhesion to the Pretender, and seeing no possibility of maintaining Theodore on the throne, he thought it best for his own safety to acknowledge the claims of Grigory Otrepieff.

Page 298. *To you Dmitry comes.* In this scene Poushkin does not follow Karamsin so closely as elsewhere. The Pretender sent messengers to Moscow with proclamations. They were seized and put into prison, the papers being burned. Thinking it very probable that his manifesto would not reach Moscow, Grigory also despatched two of his trustiest adherents, Poushkin and Plestcheff. They were brought in triumph into the city by a crowd of citizens, and the manifesto was solemnly read on the Place of Execution. The words of this proclamation are closely copied in the speech the dramatist has put into the mouth of Poushkin.

Page 303. *Dost thou hear that shriek?* On June 1, 1605, Mosalsky, Golitzine, Malchanoff, and Scheveredounoff, accompanied by three archers, murdered Theodore and his mother in their rooms at the Kremlin. The fate of Ksenia was still sadder. She was wounded, but not mortally, and by order of the Pretender, who had heard of her beauty, was brought to his house. Their deaths were announced to the people and attributed to suicide by poison, so that their bodies were buried without any funeral ceremony. The people received the news quietly and almost without a murmur. „And thus," writes Karamsin, „was accomplished God's just punishment of the murder of the true Dmitry, and thus began His fresh punishment of Russia in the accession to the throne of the false Dmitry".

www.ingramcontent.com/pod-product-compliance
Lightning Source LLC
Chambersburg PA
CBHW030007240426
43672CB00007B/863